GETTING
PUBLICITY

GETTING PUBLICITY

Martin Bradley Winston

John Wiley & Sons, Inc.
New York • Chichester • Brisbane • Toronto • Singapore

Publisher: *Judy V. Wilson*
Editors: *Dianne Littwin, Catherine Dillon*
Composition: *O. T. Productions, Inc.*

Library of Congress Cataloging in Publication Data:
Winston, Martin Bradley, 1948-
    Getting publicity.

    Includes index.
    1. Publicity. I. Title.
HM263.W593   659.2   81-16217
ISBN 0-471-08225-2   AACR2

Printed in the United States of America

82 83 10 9 8 7 6 5 4 3 2 1

To Judie, my wonderful wife, who bore with me as I gave birth to this manuscript, even as she prepared to give birth to our first born.

New Haven, Connecticut
March, 1982

Preface: Who Should Be Reading This Book?

This is a do-it-yourself book about publicity. It's intended to provide more information on how to get publicity than any one reader is ever likely to need. There's a good reason for that.

You see, we've never met. If we had a chance to discuss your needs, the budget you're working with, the time you have available to devote to publicity, and all the other details that make and shape a publicity program, then you might be reading a much shorter book. Lacking all that, it seemed prudent to approach this book with a commitment to thoroughness. So whether you're a volunteer worker with a non-profit organization or a professional businessperson with a need for additional exposure, you'll find what you need to know in the pages that follow. You'll also find at least a few things you don't need to know.

So, let's begin with a word of advice. If you should come to a section that doesn't seem to apply to what you're doing or that covers something you already know, skip it. It'll still be there later if you find you need to read it after all.

For students, charities, civic and cultural organizations, non-profit and community groups, politicians, special interest groups, advocacy organizations, and businesses large or small, publicity has proven to be an effective way of gaining important exposure and meaningful results. All of these, as well as people involved with publicity or advertising agencies, will find this to be a volume of pertinent information.

Shall we begin?

Table of Contents

The Task at Hand

You have news to share—information about things you sell, things you do, or the way you do them. You have some idea of the people you want to reach with your news. Now only the problem of how to reach them remains.

There's nothing complicated or difficult about getting publicity; nothing terribly mysterious. And there's almost nothing you need to know that isn't covered here.

But do you know what publicity is? Do you confuse it with advertising? Merchandising? Promotion? Public relations? Or any of a dozen other buzz-words in the marketing communications vocabulary? (Marketing communications is a broad term that encompasses all of these.)

We should start with a firm understanding of just what publicity is and isn't, of what it can do for you, and of the people you'll be dealing with.

In this chapter, we'll be asking and answering some very basic questions:

- What is publicity?

- What can publicity do for you?

- Is there news in what you're doing?

- Who has a need to know about you?

- What do you have to do?

What Is Publicity?

In a word, publicity is news.   But not all news results from publicity. Even the news media use a special term for news that is not generated from publicity: They call it hard news. Let's take a look at some of the end results of publicity that you're accustomed to seeing.

One of the most common forms of news generated by publicity is the brief "new product" announcement you see in magazines. Often only a few lines or a paragraph, these herald the coming of all kinds of products.   They are usually the result of a new product release—one form of news release.   News releases trigger the chain of events that results in publicity.   New cameras and accessories are seen in magazines that reach camera buffs, new electronic gadgets are seen in magazines that reach electronic hobbyists, and new cars are seen in almost everything you read, from the morning paper to magazines like *Motor Trend* and *Popular Mechanics.*

We've introduced a few terms here you may or may not be familiar with.   *Media* refers to all the places where people read or hear about news, including newspapers, magazines, television, and radio. Media, by the way, is a plural noun; any one of these is a *medium*.

A *press release*—which may also be called a *news release, publicity release,* "*blurb,*" *broadside,* or simply *release*—is a printed report used by people who want to communicate their   story   to   editors. Editors control what does or does not appear in a paper, magazine, or broadcast.   The release includes the key facts to be communicated, which may or may not include such things as product specifications, quotes from key people, when the news happened (or will happen), and whom to contact for additional information.   Often, the release will also include a photograph, since this increases its chances of being selected by the editor.   We'll be taking a more in-depth look at releases and photography a bit later.

Another form of publicity you've often seen is news of personnel appointments, transfers, and promotions.   Again, the cycle begins with a press release that is sent to one or, more often, several editors.

So publicity can be thought of as the process that takes your story to the people you want to reach, through the news and information media.

Other Forms of Marketing Communications

Before we leave the question of what publicity is, you may be interested in some   of   the   things publicity isn't—like marketing, advertising, public relations, or sales promotions. If these marketing communications terms seem confusing, read the explanation of how they differ from publicity below. It's important to understand exactly what we mean when we use the word "publicity," and to start without misconceptions.

Marketing

Marketing means influencing the behavior of one or several persons in such a manner that they will make the purchase, cast the vote, or offer the contribution desired from them. This involves convincing an audience, which in turn means communicating a message.

Advertising

Advertising isn't publicity. One difference is that you always pay for the space and time in an ad (or commercial, which is an ad appearing in one of the broadcast media—radio or television). By contrast, publicity is not generally subject to a charge for space or time by the media which run it. There are a few specific exceptions to this. Some publications routinely charge a nominal fee on some excuse or another; these are generally industrial publications, and even in these few cases, the charges are nowhere near as high as the costs of advertising.

Another difference is that you have virtually full control over the message in advertising, and the ad or commercial runs with your exact wording. In the case of publicity, the publication is under no obligation to run a story in any form; in fact the editors will generally rewrite press releases. You also have no control over when the release will run. It's all up to the editor.

We don't want to leave the impression that publicity is absolutely free—just relatively inexpensive. The costs mount with the size and aggressiveness of your program. But no matter what size program is conducted, the investment in publicity is always the most efficient investment in any marketing communications program. Even given the iffy nature of publicity, the benefits far outweigh the costs.

Public Relations

Publicity is also different from *public relations*, though publicity can play a key role in any public relations program. Public relations is exactly what the words imply—the relations of a business or, especially in the case of politics or entertainment, a personality with the public. Every company has public relations, but not every company has a public relations program.

Sales Promotion

Another thing that publicity isn't is called *sales promotion*. The object of sales promotion is to encourage increased sales volume, usually through a series of promotional devices or events aimed at producing temporarily increased sales volume. Sales promotion devices include discount coupons, rebate offers, promotional giveaways (get something free with your purchase), and self-liquidating premium offers. Self-liquidating means these offers pay their own way; it usually involves buying something at a reduced price when you send in a proof of purchase with your check. Other sales promotion events include special sales, contests, and traffic-building promotions. This last type of sales promotion is designed specifically to increase the number of people who come into a business location, like a store or a church carnival, or attend an event, like an athletic event or club meeting. It can involve personal appearances by celebrities, how-to sessions, hospitality offerings, like free coffee or ten-cent sandwiches, door prizes, and so on.

Again, publicity can be used as a tool to help communicate the basic information concerning a promotional event to the public, but publicity and promotion are not the same entity. Publicity is not marketing, advertising, public relations, or sales promotion. It is a process that communicates information to the public through the news and information media.

Is publicity what you thought it was when you bought this book? Let's hope so, or at least let's hope you can see the value of publicity itself. You may wonder if publicity is a reasonable approach to accomplishing the goals you have in mind. Or perhaps you've only begun to think about goals. Either way, we're led to the second of our basic questions about publicity.

What Can Publicity Do for You?

Since publicity communicates your messages through news and information media, all of the power of these media is brought to bear when the public—those viewers, listeners, or readers you want to reach—learns about your news. Think of what this means: high interest levels, credibility, implied objectivity, and, possibly, implied endorsement by the person reporting the information.   There's also an urgency conveyed when being reported in a current news and event medium, and a tremendously large audience, which is now aware of both you and your news.

For some of the purposes of publicity, these are an end unto themselves; for others, these are just side effects. For a better understanding of what publicity can do for you, we should look at some specific examples of what can happen when publicity releases run. Not everything we talk about happens every time, as you'll come to better understand in later chapters, but at least we'll get an introduction to some possible results.

Sales Leads

One thing that publicity can deliver is a list of the people who have not only seen your news, but who are also interested in what they've seen. Where do these "hot prospects" come from?

You may have noticed that some of the magazines you read offer "readers' service" cards, which ask the reader to circle a number in order to receive information about products that are being advertised or announced in "New Products," "Product Review," "Manufacturers' Literature" and similar columns, or feature articles, "Product Round-ups," and so on. These inquiring readers are potential customers. While some inquiries result from advertising, those prompted by the various columns, articles, and so forth are usually the result of publicity.

If your publicity is used by one of these publications offering readers' service, the result is a list of those people who have indicated interest in your product or service, compiled by the publication and delivered to you. Consider this as a valuable list of sales prospects, prequalified because they've all indicated specific interest in you and what you offer.

Awareness

Another important result of publicity—in any medium—is that it helps make people *aware* of you and what you offer. Don't underestimate the value of such awareness. A considerable volume of research compiled by advertising agencies and others for more than half a century indicates that most buyers tend to narrow their final buying decisions down to two or three candidates.   Naturally, they don't consider candidates they don't know about.   So a prerequisite to being considered at all is awareness.   You must let people know that you, too, offer what they're looking for.   Publicity is an invaluable tool in helping accomplish this, and can also communicate specific features and benefits, to help present what you offer to its best advantage.

Publicity can also help you to enter new marketplaces, to expose your products or services to new customers, and to do it without the expense of an advertising program.   Let's say, for example, that you sell baking dishes to restaurants.   With publicity, you might be able to reach hospital kitchens, school cafeterias, or gourmet cooking enthusiasts—all potential customers you normally wouldn't reach or sell to.

Publicity lets you keep more of your products and services in front of the people you do sell to as well.   Even big companies take advantage of this increased exposure by complementing their advertising exposure of one group of products with publicity exposure of another.   In fact, the more sophisticated the company, the more likely it is to keep all of its products exposed to all of its potential customers all of the time —through publicity.   This creates a constant awareness, a constant flow of information, and a constant influx of inquiries, especially when augmented with advertising and other marketing communications tools.   This strategy of coordinating campaigns among several marketing communications tools, as sophisticated as it can be, is within anyone's capabilities.   We'll be passing on advice and examples of this as we go along.

Market Research

Publicity is also capable of helping you to discover whether or not you should try to reach a new type of customer.   It does this by allowing you to gauge the response of each audience for each publication or broadcast.   For example, suppose that you sell machine screws to companies that use them to assemble equipment.   You've been thinking about expanding your marketplace (selling to new kinds of customers) by offering prepackaged assortments of machine screws: But to whom? You turn to publicity for exposure, selecting publications that reach a few specific audiences.   (These are called specific interest or special interest publications.)   These might include do-it-yourselfers, electronics hobbyists, people who run hardware stores, model railroad enthusiasts, people who work on their cars, and so on.

As the results come in (which may be in the form of inquiries, letters, or phone calls), keep a record of where each inquirer learned of you. Some publications may do well, some poorly, and this may be instantly apparent to you. If not, you can break out your pocket calculator to determine the *percentage of circulation* of each publication represented by the inquiries you receive. This, by the way, is the technique used by some of the most sophisticated publicity-based marketing researchers in the industry; they usually find that anything that pulls a response from more than a quarter of one percent of a magazine's circulation (0.25% is equivalent to 25 inquiries for every 10,000 readers) is a smashing success. Anything that draws less than a fifth of this is a dismal failure. These general rules, of course, apply to industrial publications more so than consumer publications, and are based on statistics from those that provide readers' service inquiries.

Our example, by the way, is included here to give you a hint of the power of publicity as an investigative tool. Even if you never find the need to adopt this kind of program, the fact that it can be done may suggest some other ways in which publicity can provide information.

Why Bother?

Now that you've been introduced to much of what publicity can help you accomplish, the investment you make is up to you. Remember, though, that publicity is controllable, moderate, and one of the best values of all of the many marketing communications techniques. It can take up a little of one person's time or the total commitment of a large staff, depending on the level of commitment that you decide is appropriate.

You might even want to use one of the many professional publicity agencies. Most advertising agencies, especially those that are considered full-service agencies, also provide professional publicity assistance. These professionals offer experience, expertise, and ongoing contact with key editors. But the option is yours.

Publicity programs all require some amount of time, attention, research, follow-up and good, hard work. The more you do yourself, the less out-of-pocket money you'll need to invest; the more you're willing to spend on outside services, the less of your time and energy will be required.

One way or another, publicity requires a certain group of resources, but again, it's all under your control. Your first publicity expenditure could be as inexpensive as a phone call, letter, or short release to a limited number of editors.   It's best to start small to help establish the operations and procedures while the program is still flexible and easily changed. This also gives you a chance to gain some comfort and experience without the pressures a big program can bring. Yes, it does get easier as you go along, and adding to a program is easy—certainly easier than starting from scratch.

But the real reason that most companies and organizations get involved with publicity is return on investment. Publicity helps you do what you set out to do, usually with a much smaller investment in time and energy than any other technique. An aggressive, sophisticated publicity program might require an investment equivalent to 1 to 2% of your sales volume, and almost certainly means a sales volume increase several times as large. An advertising program, by comparison, usually requires an investment of 5% of your sales volume, and might require an investment as large as 20% of your sales volume; the returns on an aggressive advertising program are also impressive, to be sure, but the size of the investment is substantially larger.

Of course, in order to reap the benefits of publicity, you have to issue releases. And many people feel that there is very little in what they do or what they offer that's important enough to warrant being published or broadcast. Which brings up our next question.

Is There News in What You're Doing?

The answer is almost always yes—or will be before you've finished this book. Sometimes the news in what you're doing is obvious. You may just be starting out in business. You may be offering a brand new product or service. You may have added a new location, or started doing business in a new area. Sometimes, of course, the "news" is a little less obvious; and, frankly, there are times when you'll be injecting the newsiness into what you report. But let's take a brief look at some of the ways there may be news in what you're doing; we'll follow up with a more detailed look in Chapters 3 and 4.

In addition to new products, you can find a variety of new aspects of products—ever-changing aspects, in many cases—that offer repeated opportunities for exposure. There are changes in price, changes in packaging, and changes in availability, to name a few. Product literature, called *collateral material*, is another area where you can find news in a not-new product. New product information sheets, catalogs, brochures, and so on offer additional opportunities for exposure.

You can also use publicity to increase the effectiveness of certain sales promotion activities by exploiting their innate newsworthiness.

Editors have often been known to run stories about contests, sweepstakes, rebates, personal appearances, in-store appearances, self-liquidating premium offers, and more.

Even though not strictly considered news, information about how products are used, called *applications information*, is often given favorable consideration by editors.   (That is, there is a good chance that they will consider it worth sharing with their readers.) Remember, we've defined publicity as concerning both news and information. But that doesn't mean that there isn't a newsy way of reporting applications information.

One way is to find out how your customers are using your products or services.   If nothing else, you may be surprised at what you learn; and, of course, if you're surprised, an editor may be interested, too. Even if you already know everything about how your customers use what you offer, there are things you can share through a release that an editor will select because he thinks his readers or listeners will be interested.   And the only new thing about your "news" is that you went to the trouble to report it.

Another way you can get news coverage of your products is to report on *very* large orders,   especially if they come from new or unusual customers.   Even the business pages of your local newspaper are likely to report this kind of news.

Personnel changes are another way of getting publicity exposure. New company officers and executives, as they are appointed or named, are one way to gain exposure.   Promotions or new responsibilities for specific personnel within the company are another.

By the way, there are times when no news is in itself newsworthy. For example, if it's been more than six months since a price increase, you could issue a release that tells how you've held the line against price increases.   If your sales on a product are either weaker or stronger than usual, you can report that in a press release—often quoting yourself or someone else within the company.

Quotes, by the way, are an easy way to get two or more releases from the same piece of   "news."   When something happens, first report it, then report a company official's remarks on it: why it happened, how it happened, what it means, and so on.

Awards are another good opportunity for publicity. This can include awards you win or those you bestow.   In fact, there are firms that create awards because of the publicity coverage they bring.   You're going to have to decide for yourself whether or not this accomplishes any of the goals you set for your own publicity program.

So all in all, it would appear that there probably is news in what you're doing, even when you wouldn't think so.   The editor   who decides whether or not your publicity release will run is the judge of that.   And the determining factor in this judgment is going to be that editor's audience—the readers, viewers, or listeners that are reached.   Which brings us to another of our questions.

Who Has a Need to Know About You?

Perhaps the best way to gain some insight into the answer to this question is to consider it from the other side of the communications channel: Of the people you interrelate with, whom do you have a need to know about?

There are your suppliers in one category, your customers in another, and your competitors in yet another.   Lawmakers whose decisions could affect the way you do business are in another category, and you can probably think of a few more yourself.

But wait a minute!   Do you want your competitors to know what you're doing?   Isn't that a dangerous aspect of publicity?   This is one area where we can go beyond the strategy of a good publicity program and discuss *tactics*.

First, you know what a disadvantage it can be to be placed in a position of having to react to a competitor and what an advantage it can be to have the initiative.   With publicity announcing your plans, your competitors don't know of them until your customers do.   It will take time for your competitors to react, and more time for their reactions to reach your (or their) customers.   You not only have the advantage in time, but you also have the advantage of placing your competition in a defensive position.   You establish yourself as the "trend-setter" in your business.

Let's take a look at what other kind of people you'll want your publicity to reach.   The primary audience for most publicity programs can be broadly classified as *customers*, a term that can take on a variety of interpretations.   If you are a manufacturer, your customers include not only end users, but all the various stages of distribution that must first buy your product for resale.   In a sense, independent factory representatives are often considered as customers too since they usually represent a number of other manufacturers, called *principals*.   You have to buy their time and attention during each sales call and the more emphasis they put on you and the more often, the more sales are likely to result.

If your company is publicly owned, the financial and investment communities are also customers of yours, since they buy, sell, and trade your company itself.   Whether or not you are publicly owned, some of this audience is nevertheless important to you, since these people are important sources of loans and financing, and you have to sell them on the ongoing success, prosperity, profitability, and liquidity of your company.

In another sense, you have concepts you need to sell to the lawmakers who could make the laws and rules under which you operate either a little harder or a little easier to comply with.   While these are not strictly customers, the broad concept of "customer" nonetheless leads us to consider these people.

Another group you constantly deal with includes your vendors and suppliers—the people you buy materials from.   The bigger, more important, and more significant you can appear in their eyes, the better the chances you have of obtaining a favorable, flexible position in bargaining with them.

Your employees are another group of people you may want to reach with publicity (among, we hope, other methods).   In addition to the benefits that good employee morale can bring to your productivity, consider some of its other potential capabilities.   A strong image of good working conditions, ongoing promotions, and good employee relations can help you attain a very favorable bargaining position when negotiating new contracts, either with individuals or with unions. And this same information can help you attract the kind of people you want most for personnel vacancies, as they occur.

Another potential audience for publicity is the community in which your business is located.   Publicity can help you present yourself as a good, concerned, involved neighbor. It can present your side of the story on community issues, and can help to solve and to prevent problems.

Once again, it is important to take the first step of deciding the goals of any publicity activity you undertake, whether it is an aggressive, sophisticated program or a single release.

To summarize, some possible goals for a publicity program include:

1. Gain competitive initiative.

2. Influence customers.

3. Influence the financial community.

4. Influence the legislative community.

5. Improve employee relations.

6. Improve community relations.

What Do You Have To Do?

There's a lot of work that has to be done before anybody can read about what you're doing. Even the least organized, most haphazard publicity effort requires that a release reach an editor. But since we want to be neither haphazard nor poorly organized, let's look at the steps involved in putting together a properly managed publicity program. This will also lay the groundwork for some of the subjects that we'll cover in future chapters.

Establishing Goals

The first and most important step in our publicity program is to formalize our goals. What missions do you want your publicity program to accomplish? Which audiences are you trying to reach? What are the returns you're trying to get? Once you've settled on the answers to these questions and others like them, put them down on paper in your own words. The goals that you set will dictate the direction your program will take. Later, when you're working hard to get things done, at least you'll have the satisfaction of knowing that you're heading the right way. To help you with the job, here are some of the specific kinds of questions you'll want to decide on:

- Whom do you want to reach? Investors? End users? Manufacturers' representatives? Distributors? Master distributors? Dealers? Vendors? Suppliers? Competitors? Colleagues? Buyers? Purchasing agents? Professional users? Casual users? Hobbyists? Traditional markets? New markets? Lawmakers?

- What action do you want them to take? Should they place an order? Contact you for more information? Contact someone else—a representative, distributor, or dealer—for more information? Attend a function? Hold you in higher esteem? Side with you politically? Support you? Defend you? Love you? Hate your competitors?

- How much do you want to invest in your program? How much of your own time? How much of anyone else's time? How much money? How much equipment?

- How will you determine the success or failure of your program? What measures will you use? Sales? Inquiries? Formal survey research from a professional specialist? Gut feeling?

- How will you follow up inquiries? Are existing materials good enough, or will you have to create new ones?

- When do you want the program to begin? Will it be a temporary company activity or an ongoing one? How visible do you want to be, which is to say, how often do you want releases to go out to any one editor? To every editor?

- Are there any other goals or limitations that you want to establish for your publicity program?

Identifying Your Targets

The second step—and all that follow—result from the goals you establish. In this case, it's determining your *universe*. This is a term used to describe the roster of all the editors you will ever want to be in contact with at any given stage in your program. You may decide that the only people you ever want to reach, for example, are dealers of model railroad equipment. There are roughly half a dozen magazines in this field, and it's unlikely that you would ever have more than twenty names on your mailing list, including every editor and major author in the field. If your company were larger, though, and your business activities more widespread, your list may eventually number in the thousands!

There are directories available at your local library that list publications of every description, giving the full particulars of their readership, their staff, and more. We'll discuss these in more detail in the next chapter.

Someone is going to have to spend time digging up the names and addresses you'll need for your mailing list, or lists. Often, in running a publicity program, you will find there are times when you want your release to reach only some of the editors in your universe. You may know that the others won't be interested or you may want only some readers—just dealers and not customers, for example—to hear what you have to say. You'll need to know which publications reach which audiences, the phone numbers of all key editors, their responsibilities, the dates of special focus issues that concern you, and more. In short, there's a lot of homework to be done in identifying the media in your universe, and in learning the specifics about them.   You can do it yourself, or you can pay an advertising or public relations agency to do it for you.

Locating Resources

You're also going to have to do some homework in identifying your best choices of where to go to get your releases written, pictures taken, quantity photos made, printing done, and so on.   Again, we'll be covering these areas in later chapters, but here's a checklist of some of the resources you will have to either provide or pay for.

1. STATIONERY.   Most companies prepare a special version of their company letterhead that includes wording like "for immediate release" or "news release."   Sometimes this extends to special envelopes as well.   You will probably want 9" x 12" or 10" x 13" envelopes to accommodate 8½" x 11" releases and 8" x 10" photos. Use a sheet of cardboard behind each photo or group of photos to act as a stiffener and prevent damage.   Stationery has to be both designed and printed; other supplies need to be purchased.

2. SUPPLIES.   At a minimum, you'll need lots of staples and index cards.   You'll probably also find yourself using a lot of file folders, typewriter ribbon, type correcting materials, notebooks, and copy masters.

3. EQUIPMENT.   While you may not need everything listed here, you'd better think about copiers, postage meters, filing cabinets, extra typewriters, duplicators, staplers, address imprinters, sorters, collaters, bundlers, and possibly a computer terminal.   If you intend to add to your staff, don't forget desks, chairs, and so on.   And you might want to take a good look at your telephone equipment, especially the number of lines and extensions you have. You may even decide to add a customers' toll-free number to handle inquiries, though this is a considerable expense.

4. WRITERS.   Someone is going to have to write these releases. Is it you?   If not, you'll need the services of a writer;   either someone on staff, someone at an agency, or a freelancer (we'll explain these options later).   If the person who ultimately manages your publicity program

isn't the person who writes the releases, there's going to have to be some review and approval procedure implemented. Otherwise, you might be placing your company in the peril of possible public embarrassment.

5. ADMINISTRATIVE MATERIALS. Releases have to be typed, often onto special master forms that permit them to then be printed directly onto news release letterhead stationery. Printing and photography have to be ordered. Envelopes must be addressed, stuffed, sealed, stamped, and mailed. Records have to be kept, both of these operations and of the inquiries that result. Inquiries have to be answered, meaning more mailing operations. If inquiries are also being referred to someone else—one of your dealers if you manufacture, for example, or one of your manufacturers if you're a dealer—this involves an additional mailing operation. The important thing is to recognize the scope of operations involved and to assign responsibilities for them. It is likely that the secretarial, sales, shipping, and mailing people you already have are not only capable of assuming these duties, but will welcome the excitement of communicating through the media and hearing back from the public.

6. PHOTOGRAPHY. You'll have to select a photographer, schedule a shooting session, have products ready for it, choose the best shot, arrange for retouching (if necessary) and, when all that's done, find someone who can have all the prints you'll need made on a price and delivery schedule you can live with. We'll have more to say about this in Chapter 6.

7. PRINTING. For a small publicity program, office copiers or duplicators can prepare your releases readily, but for any program involving 100 releases or more, you'll probably want to go to someone with an offset printing press. Either way, there's paper to buy (your letterhead or special release letterhead stationery, most likely), pages to collate and staple, and schedules to meet. And don't forget the detail of getting materials to and from the printer.

8. MAILING. Here's where much of the expense of your program will occur. Postage costs for releases, which businesses will *always* want to mail first class, can be near a dollar for each person you mail each release to. Non-profit

organizations may want to investigate special postal rates available to them, though for a slower-than-first-class delivery. Envelopes can be expensive, so you may want to consider roll-fed polyethylene envelopes as an alternative; either way, the materials have to be collected and inserted into the envelope. The address has to be reproduced and either imprinted on the envelope or on a label which is affixed to the envelope. There must be postage in the meter or stamps on hand, and the mound of mail you create has to reach the post office.

9. SPECIALS. Press conferences and media events bring other problems—arrangements for facilities, preparation of speeches and official statements, preparation of special demonstrations and exhibits, arrangements for any food or drinks you want to make available, scheduling people, sending invitations, getting confirmations, and so on.

That should give you a fairly complete picture of the work you're in for, but if you take things slowly and methodically, a step at a time, you'll find publicity isn't only easy to get, it's fun.

Don't be scared by the list you just read. As we continue, you'll find out how to accomplish each step with a minimum of aggravation. Isn't that the way you want to do it? Read on.

2

Working with the Media

Publicity's job is to make the media report stories that they might not otherwise report, or to report them a little differently. Publicity provides information not otherwise available, whether it's basic fact or opinion.

In this chapter, we're going to discuss how to "manipulate" the media. Perhaps a better term—certainly one that's more acceptable to editors and journalists—is "motivate." We'll take a look at what it is about a press release that editors look for, and what you can do to help its chances of running. We'll see how to create media interest in your story not only through the information your release contains, but also through contact with editors. And we'll try to create a better understanding of the editor's side of the publicity channel with some insight into the little things—and the big things—that editors look for.

What Does an Editor Do?

The eventual success or failure of your publicity program is going to depend substantially on how often the releases you send in are selected to run. That decision is in the hands of a person whose title is usually "editor." The editor, as we've seen, is your "opposite number," the person on the other side of the publicity channel. Understanding his or her job will help you do yours a little better.

Can you name the editor of your local newspaper? Careful, that's a trick question. Newspapers (except some very small ones) usually have many people acting as editors, usually assigned to specific types of news.   There may be business editors, fashion editors, financial editors, sports editors, hobby editors, feature editors, travel editors, entertainment editors, real estate editors, automotive editors, and food editors, to name a few.   The staff of a large daily paper in a metropolitan area might well include over a hundred editors.

Each of these editors has some additional staff, which may include reporters, critics, commentators, photographers, illustrators, and more; or, for a small, special-interest section, the editor may double in some or all of these functions.

Publicity releases are the primary source of information for most editors in all but the "hard news" areas. Usually, releases are selected, edited (meaning preened and pruned, with grammar corrected or altered into the style guidelines prescribed for the newspaper, and prepared for typesetting) or rewritten, and run.   But those are the *lucky* releases; most never see the black of ink or the light of day.

Newspapers

Conservatively speaking, most editors reject six or more releases for every one they run.   The larger the circulation of the paper, the more important the area of responsibility, the more active the field, the more releases an editor has to reject for each one that runs.

Newspapers operate on a space budget, which is not to be confused with the financial budget under which newspapers, like all other businesses, operate.   Each edition of each paper has its own space budget, which includes the total number of pages printed and the space that must be reserved for advertising. Ads, after all, pay their way and provide the newspaper with the largest portion of its income.   Each edition's remaining space is allocated to specific stories and departments in a daily *budget meeting*, attended by each of the key editors in some papers, and key managing editors in others.

The selection of press releases to appear as news is based on the personal and professional judgment of the editor, and the main influencing factor in the decision can often be stated in a single word: *newsworthiness.*

Newsworthiness

There are probably as many definitions of newsworthiness as there are editors, but we will take the initiative in stating our own.   Newsworthy stories are those that offer the most information with the most urgency to the most people.

Just because today's release isn't in tomorrow's paper doesn't always mean it won't be run at all.   Some releases that aren't newsworthy enough to merit coverage in a daily edition may fit in a Sunday or weekend paper, where there's usually more room.   And perhaps, if not this weekend, it may show up next week, or the one after—but rarely any later.

What happens to releases that aren't selected right away?   Sometimes they are kept for future use, though usually they hit the editor's infamous "file thirteen," the wastebasket.

Magazines

Magazines operate very much like newspapers, with departments, editors, and budget meetings.   But magazines differ in a few important ways.

For one, the potential life span of a release is much longer.   A monthly magazine, for example, might not run the release you send for six to eight months.   When they do run it, of course, it's in front of its readers for the full month of the issue instead of just one day. Depending on the printing and preparation schedule, that same release could appear as soon as a week or two after you send it.

The editorial focus and format of a magazine are usually more specialized than those of a newspaper.   "Focus" refers to the subjects a magazine covers; these might include news for magazines like *Newsweek*, the financial world for magazines like *Fortune*, ham radio for magazines like *Ham Radio,* cars for magazines like *Motor Trend*, personal computers for magazines like *Byte,* adult entertainment for magazines like *Playboy,* science fact and fiction for magazines like *Omni*, home economics for magazines like *Woman's Day*, and so on. "Format" refers to the way in which a magazine's news and information features (called "editorial material") are presented.

There are a number of magazines that exist primarily as a showcase for new products, services, and product literature.   These magazines are invariably good producers of readers' service inquiries, and they tend to print more publicity-release-generated information than other publications.   The product showcase format is one you'll learn to look for because of its excellent reputation for producing results.

Most special interest publications—those that focus on limited, well-defined audiences who share a specific interest in a given hobby, personal activity, business activity, or professional interest—also include at least one product showcase section.   However, since it has to be smaller than the product showcase coverage of an all-showcase publication, the chances of your release appearing here are also smaller.   The more specific the special interest of a magazine, the smaller its circulation is likely to be;   this more select audience, of course, also means fewer extraneous readers.

Magazines with very large circulation (more than half a million readers) or very small circulation (less than 10,000 readers) are less likely to offer readers' service.   Even without readers' service, however, your company's name, address, and phone number will usually be included in the printed item that results from your release, so readers will be able to contact you.

General interest publications are those that do not try to reduce their readership by any specific focus;   in fact, they often try to increase readership by presenting an attractive format.   Examples of general interest publications include *Readers' Digest, People, Life,* and *Us.*   General interest publications are usually very large, with circulations in the millions.   They almost never offer readers' service. Still, the editors of these magazines—keenly aware of their audience and its interests—are constantly on the lookout for publicity items that might make good reading.   Your chances of appearing in these publications are very slim, but with the size of audience they offer, the potential rewards are extraordinary.

Whether special interest or general interest, the closer your release relates to the audience of a publication and the greater its impact on that audience, the more likely that an editor is going to accept it.

Once again, the selection is made on the basis of its newsworthiness to the reader.   An editor is most interested in his or her readers. The more interested they are in what you have to say and the more timely the information you communicate, the better.   The release offering *the most information with the most urgency to the most people* in the publication's audience is the one that an editor will select first every time.

Broadcasting

Exactly the same kind of decisions of newsworthiness face the people who work in broadcasting. But let's hold the discussion of similarities off for a moment as we take a closer look at the differences.

There are several categories of programs that we will want to consider.   These include news broadcasts, public affairs programs, educational programs, informational programs, and entertainment programs.

Television Newscasts

News broadcasts on television stations are quite different from those on radio. Television news is primarily conducted in two programs of approximately 30 minutes at 10:00 P.M. or 11:00 P.M., and from 30 to 90 minutes at the dinner hour, some time between 5:30 and 7:30. There may also be mid-day lunch hour reports, generally 30 minutes in length, brief sign-on and sign-off reports (5 to 15 minutes), and perhaps one or two more news broadcasts during the broadcast day. Each newscast tries to be independent of the others, for the most part, while repeating at least headlines and salient aspects of key stories.

The term newscast, of course, refers to the entire program time, during which there are news reports, sports reports, special features, special reports, and commercials. Each 30-minute program might include 6 minutes of news, 4 minutes of special reports, 4 minutes of weather, 5 minutes of sports, 3 minutes of special features, 1 minute of program opening and closing themes, and 7 minutes of commercials and station identification announcements.

Television news, you see, operates on a time budget, much as magazines and newspapers operate on a space budget. In television it's called a schedule, timetable, script, format, or guide. The person who decides what goes into each block each day and how much time it is allotted is called the news producer—the equivalent of a magazine or newspaper editor. Television newsrooms also include an editor or two: the assignment editor, who makes sure that reporters, camera personnel and technical personnel are assigned to each story; and, in some larger newsrooms, a copy editor, who reviews each reporter's script copy to make sure that the story is presented grammatically correctly, fairly, and completely. Often, a reporter will be his own editor, with the assignment editor or news producer acting as the overall quality control checkpoint.

Most stories covered by television newscasts are chosen on the basis of impact on the viewing audience, urgency, and visual impact. If the choice comes down to two stories of equal impact and urgency and one offers more exciting, graphic pictures, that will count strongly in its favor. Also, with the extremely short deadlines of "instant" news (I have been in newsrooms where stories were written *after* the newscast began and run into the studio during a commercial break or even while the camera was on another reporter), the station's ability to get people and equipment to where the story is happening can be a determining factor.

Hard news stories—reports on crimes, accidents, major legislative, judicial, or executive actions, and similar news events—always get first preference.   And the average length of a television news report at a competitive station is between 20 and 25 seconds!   In fact, only special features, investigative reports, or special focus reports are ever given more time for a story.

The chances of your publicity release being newsworthy enough to survive the rigors of this grueling regimen are slim, but it can be done. One way is through press conferences, press demonstrations, and a special category of publicity called the "media event."   (We'll cover these in more depth in Chapter 4.)

A "media event" is any presentation made to a live audience in which the primary intention is to provide material of interest to the news media, who are, for the purposes of the media event, the most significant part of that audience.   In other words, media events are the newest version of the publicity stunt, usually more legitimate, to be sure, than the term "stunt" would imply, designed to cater to the needs of the news media by providing the urgency,   information, interest, and pictorial impact that help any story make the news.

Radio Newscasts

On radio, newscasts are even more rigorous, usually offering just 3 to 5 minutes each hour.   There's almost never time for much more than the headlines and key features of the day's top stories on radio, though a media event can increase the odds of your story making it on the air. The people in control of radio news are usually called "news directors," although many news staffers exert some independence in their story selection.

Some radio stations offer expanded news coverage during afternoon drive time (primarily 5:00 to 6:00 P.M.) with newscasts lasting from 15 minutes to half an hour.   The chances of your news running are greater here than at any other time of day; in fact, the chances of your story running in a 30-minute radio newscast are greater than in a 30-minute television newscast.   There are more *actualities* (on-the-scene reports) on television, which consume more time, whereas most radio news is delivered as a reading of a prepared story.

Your best chance of all of having a story appear during a newscast happens with an all-news format radio station.   Forty-six or more minutes each hour (the balance being allotted to commercials) are devoted to news, sports, weather, special reports, and special feature coverage.   These stations operate more like a magazine or newspaper, with more departments, more editors and producers, more reporters, and more time available.   Their biggest interest is in those stories that will attract the biggest interest of the biggest part of the community—their listening audience—over the course of an hour or a day. Since your story affects some part of the community, they will be predisposed to include it, if at all possible.   But, again, they require the same qualities of *newsiness* that all media demand, and in addition, they require that there be no mistaking your announcement for a commercial or promotional message.

Talk Shows

There are programs on radio and television that cater to the audience's interest in keeping informed on a variety of topics. Chief among these is the talk show or interview show, which permits product demonstrations, a sharing of skills and techniques, interviews with interesting, engaging or influential people, and so on.   While the hosts of the programs generally act as interviewers and moderators, these programs often provide opportunities for members of the audience to phone in their questions and comments.

For these programs, there is often an assistant producer who is assigned the function of lining up interesting guests, in addition to a producer who coordinates the overall effort. Both mail and telephone contact with an assistant producer can prove rewarding.   The host, interviewer, moderator, or star of the program may or may not have the say-so as to who appears, and unless instructed otherwise, you're better off not contacting anyone other than a producer or assistant producer at first.

Public Affairs Programming

The Federal Communications Commission (FCC) is the official United States Government   administrator   of   the   rules   and   regulations governing broadcasters.   Chief among these is the requirement that a station operate in the public interest, convenience, and necessity. Broadcasters are required to survey their communities to determine whether or not issues affecting significant   parts of the community have been adequately and fairly addressed.   Generally, key community, civic, social, and religious leaders are consulted, individual citizens surveyed, and public comments invited. This process is called *ascertainment*. We mention it here because it helps you understand the importance of the public affairs operations of any station.

Public affairs programs are those which are expressly intended to maintain the station's role as a responsible and active participant in issues involving its viewing community. Usually, the station is delighted to take a strong role in the public interest, convenience, and necessity. There are some stations, however, that provide this kind of programming only minimally, and only to keep out of trouble when the FCC reviews their conduct at license renewal time.

The public affairs director is the individual responsible for all programming that is designed as a part of its fulfillment of its community responsibilities. If your news has an effect on the community, the public affairs directors of your local stations will go out of their way to help you share it with their audiences. Examples of this kind of news include minority employment, affirmative action programs, special training programs open to the community at large, charitable activities, and community involvement programs.

The public affairs director may also want to refer you to the producer or assistant producer of a specific program. This is very similar to being referred to a specific department editor in a magazine or newspaper.

By the way, newspapers do a significant amount of coverage of these same public affairs topics, and shouldn't be ignored. Often, a special features editor may get involved in providing longer, more substantial coverage of important stories. This is one area where *importance* to the reader outweighs *urgency* in the assessment of the story's newsworthiness. These stories may appear in any edition of the paper, but more often appear in weekend or Sunday editions or in a special magazine section.

Selling the Story

We've already seen that editors have to know what interests their readers. Often, this comes from a strong identification with the readers, which develops into an almost paternal attitude. Editors are constantly making decisions about what readers, viewers, or listeners will or won't see or hear—that's their job. Part of this judgment is based on what an editor feels the audience is already interested in and on what he or she feels the audience *should* be interested in.

And remember, the point of view of each editor is as unique as that editor's own personality and readership. If an automaker in Detroit were to develop a $1,000 car that seats six, is totally safe, and gets 100 miles to the gallon, there's no questioning the newsworthiness of its announcement.   But think of how differently the story would be told to the audiences of *Motor Trend, Business Week, Iron Age,* the *CBS Evening News, The Wall Street Journal,* the *Detroit Free Press, Advertising Age,* and *Popular Mechanics.* The same story, the same group of press releases, the same basic information can trigger as broad a spectrum of responses as there are editors and audiences.

Partly, this is because the role of media has never been confined to reporting news, but has expanded to include analyzing and interpreting. It's important to mention that because publishing and broadcasting are businesses, and business people strive for profit and profitable operations, and entertainment sells better than pure information, editors keep an ear cocked for stories that hold some potential for amusement.   When Bob Hope introduced Spiro Agnew at an Ohio State University graduation ceremony years ago by saying "his library just burned down. . . destroying both volumes . . .including the one he hadn't finished coloring yet . . . ." the story made it onto wire services and broadcasts across the country.   Is it news? Is it newsworthy?

The answer is no, it isn't newsworthy, but yes, it is news. And the only reason that it was news was that editors chose to include it with other information that was reported.

So in our understanding of newsworthiness, perhaps we ought to acknowledge that it's a very good but nevertheless imperfect indicator of "spaceworthiness."   And the difference lies in the seemingly arbitrary selection of stories made by an editor.

Editors, being journalists, preach and abide by the W-W-W-W-W-H tradition of reporting:

> the *who* . . .
>
> the *what* . . .
>
> the *where* . . .
>
> the *when* . . .
>
> the *why* . . .
>
> and the *how* of a story.

But there's more here than meets the mind at first impression. Because the way the *who, what, when, where, why,* and *how* of a story are presented is a crucial key to its being accepted by an editor as newsworthy for his or her particular audience.

Who

For you, the *who* refers both to the individual you quote in your release, if any, and the company the release is coming from—your company.   If the individual or the company is strong, influential, sizable, or for any other reason speaks with authority, credibility, and importance *on the subject of the release*, you have a much better chance of getting it selected (assuming the subject of the release is itself of interest to the editor).

So if your press release has something to do with widgets, being a leading widget manufacturer or a leading widget customer works in your favor.   If you're a manufacturer, whether or not you dominate the market, a quote from a key company officer who is also an officer on the widget manufacturers' association industry committee (or whatever your industry or trade association is called) adds clout to what is said.   Of course, the editor has to have some other reason to be interested in your news, but all things being equal, the bigger and more influential the individual and the company, the better the chances of the release being run. Or, to put it another way, play from strength.

What

The *what* is the subject of the release—a new product, a price increase, a new plant, a promotion, an official reaction, or any thing or happening you choose to announce.   As you might expect, the usual, predictable, humdrum announcements about routine price changes or promotions have a lot less chance of being run than the unusual.

For example, is there a story behind the story? If you're announcing a new location, is there something about a former tenant or resident that might add some pizzazz to the story?   Are you putting your new plant up on an old Indian hunting ground?   A stage coach route?   A haunted house site?   Anything you can do to make your story a little out of the ordinary is likely to be viewed favorably as a refreshing change of pace.

Do you have a new product?   Fine, but how new is it?   What's really different about it?   One way to be different is to make the product sound like a happy or lucky accident.   While trying to build a better mailbox, for example, did the designer discover a better way to make a hinge?   If the mailbox is the product, the story isn't unusual; but if the hinge is the new product, this "happy accident" approach gives the story some "oomph."

Or perhaps you have a price advantage, even if it's only temporary, when your product comes out.   A release that offers the headline "XYZ Company Admits Pricing Goof on New Widget" is going to get more attention than one that says "XYZ Company Announces New Widget."   Again, the "happy accident" formula helps give interest to your release.

If the *what* of your story is a personnel promotion, look for some human interest in either the person or the move.   If the move signifies a rapid rise for the individual, you might have a superior either confirm or deny that something nonsensical like being born on the planet Krypton or marrying the boss's daughter had anything to do with it.   (Careful though about being too unusual too often—if an editor thinks you're not taking the publicity channel seriously, you can be shut out of a lot more than the one release.   Perhaps the employee being promoted is a Scoutmaster or a former Eagle Scout.   If he attributes his success in business to some aspect of his outside activities, at least in part, you can again escape the commonplace to give your release that extra little boost that can make the difference between running and not running.

If the *what* of your release is an event, you're already one step ahead.   Editors see events as having more urgency than other announcements, at least partly because they're easier to position in time and usually more transient.   An event which isn't transient, like a change-from-now-on, is considered an announcement rather than an event.

If you run a store and decide to hire a petting zoo to attract children and their parents as a weekend traffic-building promotion (as one example), the chances are good that a small or suburban paper might be encouraged to announce it as news.   But your chances of getting better coverage in bigger media improve if you add a touch of the unusual—like taking the petting zoo to a local orphanage so those kids, too, can enjoy it.   Chances are that if you let the media know what you're doing four or five days in advance, you'll get some good picture coverage.   And if you take it to the orphanage a few days before you have it at your store, the petting zoo story on television, in the papers, or on the radio can prove a very powerful ally in firing up local interest—and traffic—for your promotion.

Another example: If you run a grocery, a sale on dog food is pretty ho-hum.   But if you work with your local animal shelter and offer dog food at half price (or some small amount free) to people who adopt a dog during your promotion (probably in conjunction with a coupon promotion for the rest of your customers), the chances are good that the local media will be much more interested in the story. Again, the unusual outpowers the usual.

And in-store events can be taken outdoors for even more interest. I am reminded of a seafood restaurant in the Midwest that was trying to achieve some notoriety on a limited budget. They sponsored a lobster race, inviting local media celebrities (columnists, disk jockeys, and newsmen) to pick a lobster and—with interest at a peak and cameras rolling—race it along a police-barricaded block outside the restaurant. The event not only appeared on virtually every local station and in all the papers, it was even picked up by the wire services and reported in *Sports Illustrated.* Not bad for a race where both winners and losers eat the contestants!

Where

The *where* of your release—as the example above demonstrates— can also play a key role. As you progress in the world of publicity, you'll appreciate more and more the role that staging has to play. If you're announcing a ball-bearing that reduces friction, you could take the obvious route and issue an announcement from the factory. But how much more striking a story it might be if the announcement were to be made at a gas station (playing on the more miles-per-gallon angle), an auto museum (playing on the innovation of the advancement), or a roller skating rink (playing on the simplicity yet universal appeal and application of the product category).

If you manufacture or sell shoes and have an announcement to make, get away from where you usually do business and go to where the feet are: a military or marching band practice field, a podiatry school, a dance studio, or somewhere else you might think of. And again, avoid the usual in favor of the unusual.

When you're planning a release, it's a good policy to keep yourself aware of events or activities that are upcoming within a reasonable distance to see if you might not borrow some interest from them.

For example, if you've done something to cut your overhead that results in an energy savings (or, conversely, if you've cut back on your energy usage in order to trim your overhead expenses), you can announce the fact from a hotel that is hosting an energy conference or at a utility company's shareholders' meeting. If you're introducing a new computer-related device, you can do it near a meeting of CPAs, an exhibition of antiques, a graduation ceremony, a meeting of educators, or someplace else that demonstrates by contrast the intelligence or usefulness of your product. Here, the idea is to be unusual and unexpected in an ambience that enhances your uniqueness. By comparison, the same product announcement at a computer show would be much less unusual.

If you're a restaurant or grocery owner, the best place to announce specials on pickles and ice cream may be a maternity ward, maternity clothing store, or diaper service.   If you sell toy boats and have a new product to announce, do it at a yacht club.   If you sell impact-cushioning packaging materials, announce your next product from a henhouse or egg processing facility.   Bathtubs can be announced from a dairy. (Possibly with a model taking a milk bath—yes, in a bathing suit—as we'll discuss in our chapter on photography.)   A new pork-free sausage can be introduced outside a rabbinical school or at a pig farm.   Fake fur clothing—the zoo, of course.

The point again is to provide by contrast the unusual, the unique, the unexpected;   to provide reason for an editor to take notice, to arouse a wry or dry sense of humor or irony;   to provide a story an audience will read.

When

The same contrast can be an important part of the *when* of your release or story.   Beach fashions always get more coverage when introduced at fashion shows in the dead of winter, especially if you can convince your models to wear them outside in the snow.   If you make shower heads, shower massages, or shower stalls, the first week in April seems a great time to introduce new products ("April showers").   Mutton, woolens, products aimed at sheep raisers, and so on, can be introduced as March goes out ("like a lamb").   Perhaps the headline might read,   "March comes in like a lion, goes out with light-weight woolens fashion show."

If you sell burglar alarms, watch the papers for rashes of burglaries or burglary cases coming to trial.   Similarly, big fires can help raise interest in smoke detectors, fire extinguishers, garden hoses, and more.

There's no reason to wait for once-a-year seasons and events to provide an unusual *when* for your release.   The newspapers are full of events that can provide a background contrast for your announcement.   Criminal court cases (and crimes themselves, when crimes of a specific type dominate the news for any length of time) help add to the newsworthiness of crime-prevention products and services, books about crime (either mysteries and detective stories or how-to security and protection information), self-defense classes, insurance, lighting, and more.   News about the economy helps frame a background for your news about price changes, no-changes-in-price, and new ways to use something that's already around.   Medical   and scientific discoveries can have a bearing on food and other products. Oil price increases can provide an opportunity to promote new shop-by-phone and shop-by-mail options for customers, new store locations ("we're trying to come closer to our customers so they don't have to travel as far"), and new product line offerings ("one-stop shop-ping"). Even fads can provide a tie-in: When Americans began buying rocks as pets, everyone from rock-and-roll radio stations, to bakeries offering pet rolls, to jewelers, to quarries jumped on the publicity bandwagon.

To digress for a moment, there's another aspect to the *when* of a release that's important. This is *when* it reaches the editor, or *when* it's scheduled to happen. If an editor learns of your 11:00 A.M. press conference at 9:30 A.M., you can count on not getting it covered. If your news happens Saturday evening, you can count on no reporters being available to cover it. If your news happens on election day, you can count on there being no room for it in the editor's budget. Timing can be critically important, but bad timing is easy to avoid.

The first rule is to always provide a reasonable amount of advance notice. Two days is an absolute minimum most of the time, a week more prudent. This is for the fast-break media, like radio, television newscasts, and newspapers. For magazines, the minimum is from one to two weeks in most cases, with an additional week or two being best.

The second rule is to use your common sense and avoid scheduling releases for times when you know an editor will be swamped. Election days are the worst. Holidays can be nearly as bad. And previously scheduled special events, like a convention in town, can also mean trouble. Avoid those times when the editor is working with no staff or a skeleton crew. Generally, weekday business hours are best, especially the hours between 9:30 A.M. and 2:00 P.M., which gives the reporter time to write the story and meet his daily deadline for a next edition. Also, Mondays and Fridays are somehow always more difficult than Tuesday through Thursday, but don't be afraid to ask around to see if editors in your community have any "good" or "bad" days in a week.

By the way, never ask an editor to confirm that someone will cover your event. The editor won't appreciate the pressure, and there's no way to be certain. One of my very first press conferences (I was still in college) was perfectly scheduled, but as luck would have it, the town it was held in experienced a terrible flood that morning. And Mother Nature has more clout with the media than any of us, alas.

So the third rule of timing is that once you've done your best to avoid bad timing, there are still no guarantees. You may hit it lucky and be one of the big events of a "slow news day," or you may be left high and dry when the river starts making house calls.

Why

So far we've discussed who your news is about, what it is, and where and when to schedule it.   Now, in discussing the *why* of your story, we're going to have to divide the question into two with hopes of getting a single answer.   First, *why* did your news come to pass, and second, *why* should an editor (or the readers, listeners, or viewers) find it newsworthy?

Unless there's something compellingly newsworthy about your specific *who, what, when,* or *where* (almost anything about the President, a visit by little green men from Alpha Centauri, the last day of a war, or someone doing something on the moon is newsworthy), the why of a story is the single most compelling factor available to an editor in determining its newsworthiness.   Why is it important to the audience?   Why do they want or need to know about this?   Why is this unusual or out of the ordinary?   Why is it of special interest to anyone?

Almost any action can be analyzed in terms of either its cause or its effect, and the more you can relate these to an editor and his or her audience, the better chance your story has of running.   If a price increase is caused by an increase in the cost of materials, an increase in the cost of overhead, a new labor contract which brings higher labor expenditures, increased wastage, increased handling (especially when the extra handling results from new regulations or legal requirements), new channels of distribution, increased transportation costs, or improvements in your products or services, giving the editor even just those few words of insight can help make your story more newsworthy than a simple price increase announcement. In fact, if you can acknowledge these factors *as they occur* without waiting until prices actually go up, you increase the newsworthiness of each release, while preparing the reader for a price increase.   And if acknowledging these potentially price-increasing factors seems a bad idea at first, consider this: If you announce an intention to hold your prices steady for some minimum time (30, 60, or 90 days, perhaps), you can increase your sales volume during this period by the simple mechanism of customer wanting to buy before prices go up.

Similarly, if your prices are not changing, or if they're going down, telling an editor why that's happening, and why it's either expected or, better still, unexpected, can increase the newsworthiness of your story.

The same principle holds true for simple announcements of new personnel and personnel promotions.   Why was there a vacancy? Why was this candidate selected to fill it?   Adding either or both bits of information to a simple announcement increases the chances of your announcement running, even if it ends up running with your "why" edited out.   Again, think cause and effect.   What caused the vacancy?   What effect will the new person in it have on the company?

Suppose you're announcing a new product.   Why is it any better than the old product?   Why is yours any different or better than your competitor's?   Just being there as an option, being closer to many customers, having better deliveries, offering different distribution, costing less, and so on, are valid reasons, all other things being equal.   Why would anyone buy one of these things?   In short, why does a reader need to know about this new product?

Analyze your own motives and opportunities in answering these questions, as well as those of your potential customers and the various media audiences.   What caused you to decide to offer this product? What effect will it have on the marketplace?   What caused you to select its various features and options?   What effect will they have on a buyer's decision?

There is a sophisticated rule in advertising that is simply stated: DON'T PROMOTE FEATURES, PROMOTE BENEFITS.   A feature is any specific aspect of a product or service which helps make it unique;   features belong to products.   A benefit is an advantage the user enjoys by selecting a specific product;   benefits belong to users. So what a product does or how it does it are nowhere near as meaningful as *why* there's some advantage or benefit to the user.

A pocket calculator that's promoted as "low-current CMOS and LCD technology" (features) might better be promoted by saying "batteries last a year or longer even with normal, everyday use" (benefit).   A label may be "pressure sensitive" (feature), but "peel and stick"   (feature with implied benefit) is better, and "eliminates the bother of licking or wetting" (benefit) is better still.   For a food, "naturally sweetened without sugar" (feature with implied benefit) is okay, but   "promotes tooth decay less than similar products   that are sugar-sweetened" (benefit) is better; but it had better be true.

So in describing the why of a new product, don't ignore its features, but do present them in the context of their benefits to the user.   By now, you recognize that by relating to the user you do a better job of relating to the reader.   You're therefore more newsworthy and worthy of the editor's attention.

If the what of your release is an event, the questions you'll need to answer are: Why now? Why you? Why would anyone want to come?   Why are you doing it?   And why is "why you're doing it" important?

If your event is related to a charitable activity, for example, explain the significance of the charity and of your involvement with it.   Perhaps it's helping cure an affliction that strikes children or large numbers of people, or in some other way evokes the interest of significant parts of an audience.   Should someone in the company (or someone close to someone in the company) have a personal stake, tell about it, tastefully.   Again, by going beyond a simple announcement, you can greatly enhance the interest and newsworthiness of an item.

If your event relates to company operations (the opening of a new facility or the launching of a new program, for example), tell why you've decided to do it and why it's important.   Share the causes and anticipated effects.   Don't leave the editor wondering "So what?"

How

Cause and effect and explaining why your news is happening will very naturally lead into the *how* of your story.   How did this come to pass?   How are you accomplishing this?   How did you decide? How will you cause it to happen?   How will it affect people?

Answering the *how* questions will often bring you into two specific publicity activities: providing background and documenting speculation.

A release package (see Chapter 5) can help answer the *how* questions by providing both background information and a forum for speculation.   The backgrounding function is easy to grasp, but what do we mean by *speculation?*

Sharing Speculation

Only rarely can a news medium ask and attempt to answer the question, "What does this mean in terms of the story's impact on the near and far future?"   Columnists and commentators may live forever in the world of analysis and interpretation, but reporters seldom vary from the facts of the matter, with just a "pinch" of background information to help place the story in its proper context.   It isn't the reporter's role to speculate on the impact a story might have on someone's life or lifestyle in the days or years to come.

But it is the reporter's role to share with readers the relevant specific aspects of the story that most affect them.   And if someone connected with the story is willing to share with the reporter thoughts and speculation on the impact of the announcement—well, that's often as valid an item of news as the announcement itself. Given that this "source" is willing to be identified and quoted on the record, these statements are a part of the raw material from which the reporter will draw in writing the story.

For really important events—you'll recognize them instantly on their own merits—you'll want to invest a great deal of time and energy into organizing and presenting all the relevant information you can gather. But don't overdo it. If you gather too much information, or include too much that's irrelevant, you could overwhelm the press to the point of little or no coverage.

When preparing a complex story, whether as a release package or a single release, it's important to clearly identify its main points. You have to organize your facts—and perhaps reorganize them—until understanding and appreciating your news are incidental to reading it.

Photographs

We are nearly through with our discussion of how to motivate an editor into selecting a publicity release. We've seen what information to include in our releases, and how to present it to its best advantage. We've learned the importance of staging and timing. But for all of that, our discussion of releases has been decidedly one-dimensional because we haven't said a word about anything but words. Before we leave this subject, we should focus some of our attention on the pictures that help, often more than anything else, to make our releases vibrant, meaningful, interesting, and often fascinating or exciting.

First and most important to motivating the media is the fact that almost every editor will pick a release with a picture over a release without a picture, all other things being equal.

Pictures do a great job of capturing a reader's attention—a much better job than words alone can do. And if the picture and its caption can communicate the essence of your story, so much the better. You see, not only do more readers see pictures and read captions than read stories, readers also remember pictures better and longer. And stories with pictures are read more often than stories without pictures, which is one reason editors prefer them. Another reason is that pictures help break up the all-gray look of a page that's mostly type-set words, and editors are very sensitive to the look of a page.

Pictures also add a sense of reality to a piece of information. In announcing a new product and discussing its attributes, a picture can help give form to the concepts that your words are trying to convey.

If your product is a new style telephone, for example, hearing about it is not nearly as effective as seeing it.

Creating News from "Olds"

You may realize by now that there's absolutely no reason for publicity to be dull.   The more you apply your imagination to it, the more exciting it will be.   And the more exciting and imaginative your publicity is, the more likely an editor is to select it.   Editors don't like dullness any more than the rest of us, and a lot of dull publicity releases cross their desks every working day.

So if you want to manipulate the media, motivate the media. And the way to motivate the media is to use your imagination and be creative.   One of the frustrations of publicity-seeking people is that if nothing's new, there's no reason to issue a release; but if a release isn't issued, where will publicity come from?

The first-ever release announcing a new product, service, or event is easy to write.   And with a few insights, you'll understand how to find news value even after that first-ever release, making those "bonus" releases just as easy to write as the first.   Even day-to-day routines and products that seem to offer more of the same old thing provide opportunities for new releases, if only you know where to look.

So let's take a closer look at some of the "ordinary" aspects of the products or services you'd normally be dealing with.   You'll want to see if there's a fresh side to what seems to be old news.

Changes

Have there been any actual changes in the products or services you deal with?   Even if the answer is no, you may have an angle for a story.   But if the answer is yes, the story will stand a slightly better chance of being picked up by the editors who see it.   Here are some of the places you should look for changes, and some hints on how to make their announcement a little more interesting.

Price

A permanent change in price will almost always warrant a few lines somewhere, most often in trade publications dealing with your parti-

cular product or service.   But you can usually get more than a few
lines if you explain why the price went up.   Are the raw materials
more expensive?   Is there an event that caused the raw materials to
be more expensive?   Less expensive?   A strike, a drought, an import
duty, federal controls, federal deregulation, taxes, and shortages are
often reasons behind increased material prices;   each is capable of
adding news value to your announcement.   Is labor more expensive?
Less expensive?   Why?   Again, you can borrow some news value
from the state of the economy or your company's labor relations.
Is delivery more expensive or less expensive?   Why? Does the change
in price reflect new costs or new savings due to volume, production
techniques, or the way in which your product or service is bought
and sold?

There's a lot of potential news value in the story behind the story
of an announced price increase, and it's often in your best interest
to dig for the reasons it's happening.   If prices are going down, you'll
want to make sure every possible potential customer knows about it
before he decides from whom to buy.   In the long term, this will
also help position your company as a cost-conscious, economical source
of your particular product or service.   If prices are going up, you'll
want to make sure that your potential customers understand that
there's a legitimate reason for it,   and that you're not   arbitrarily
increasing your own profits.

For example, we all realize that the price of gasoline is increasing
tenfold during the '70s and '80s.   If not for the news generated by
shortages, rationing, OPEC, and the oil industry explaining the reasons
for the price hikes, there would be a great deal more consumer resentment (not that there isn't a great deal in any case).

So it's important to share the cause behind the effect.   Look for
cause-and-effect relationships any time you prepare a release.   They
help make releases both more newsworthy and more interesting,
prime considerations when an editor sits down to decide which releases
will run and which won't.

Availability

If you offer a service primarily to people in the immediate area, any
major change in the availability of the service is going to be of interest
to them (but not necessarily to an editor).   Are you increasing your
staff to decrease customer waiting time?   Expanding your hours of
operation?   Reducing them?   Adding store locations?   Changing
the territory you cover?   Adding pick-up and delivery service?   Adding

drive-through, drop-off service?   Any of these changes in your avail-ability are reason enough to warrant issuing a release, but we're going to have to go a step further to make the news interesting enough to warrant coverage by the local media.   And non-commercial enough, because if your news sounds too self-serving, an editor will rightfully judge it more fitting for advertising than for publicity.

To find the key to the newsworthiness of your change in availability, start by looking at the reasons behind the changes.   Again, look for cause and effect. If you provide chimney sweeping service, you might cite a trend in new housing to include fireplaces more often, a greater public awareness of the role of your service in fire safety, or some other consideration that reflects a change in the habits of the general public.   Instead of headlining your release "Chimney sweep service expands hours," try focusing on these changes in buying habits with something like "Housing and fire safety trends force local chimney sweep service to expand hours."

While we've used a local service as our first example, the same, of course, is true of products and services at every level.   Have you had to make an industrial product available through retail outlets to meet consumer demand?   Have you added a telephone ordering or mail ordering operation to keep your product available (or to keep your order traffic at a reasonable level) at a time when customers are driving less? Has there been any change in order backlogs? Turnaround time? Sales outlets? Anything?

Again, look for some phenomenon that affects a large number of people, particularly a large segment of the audience reached by the specific publications or media you choose, as the cause behind the effect (change in your availability).   Use that as the focus of your headline and a large part of the substance of your release.   Here are some examples of headlines that illustrate this approach:

"Increased do-it-yourself repair activity prompts industrial manufacturer to make goods available through hardware chain."

"New interest in energy savings reason behind new 24-hour telephone information service."

"Population boom in (new location) attracts new store (or office or territory expansion) opening from (your company)."

"Normal waiting time for (product or service) cut from (what-ever) to (whatever) by (your company)."

"Reduction in personal driving cited as reason for new mail-order service from (company)."

Remember, the editor's job is to share urgent or interesting news with the reader, not to service publicity sources. Make it easy to see why readers will be interested in the news you have to share and you'll increase the odds of your release being run.

Features Vs. Benefits

Have there been any changes in the details of your product or service? The change of a detail, of one or several features, of the materials selected, of color (sometimes), or of weight can all be reasons for issuing a press release.

Is a handgrip now molded instead of smooth?   Is the power plug now a 3-prong grounded type instead of a 2-prong?   Does internal lubrication last longer?   Has there been a change in labeling?   Of recipe?   Of freshness or newness?   Here, we'll take a little turn from the cause-and-effect sermon to emphasize the difference between features and benefits: Remember, a feature is some aspect of the form or function of a product or service, while a benefit is the advantage to its user that a feature imparts.   A molded handgrip is a feature, less operator fatigue and greater control are benefits.   A 3-prong plug is a feature, reduced electrical shock hazard is a benefit.   Longer-lasting internal lubrication is a feature, less required attention to maintenance is a benefit.

Normally, of course, these are spelled out in the first announcement of any new product or service, but changes of minor features that leave a product otherwise unchanged (for example, a new drip-proof nozzle on a tube of glue, a new no-stick, see-through package for grocery store meats, a new non-glare finish on a keyboard, or a new child-proof cap on a bottle) might escape everyone's attention if you're not alert.   And that's too bad, because features like these often add to the benefits of a product without adding to its price,   meaning clear-cut extra value for the buyer and good competitive positioning for you.   But again, the thing that's going to capture an editor's eye is what's of most direct interest to most readers;   in this case, the extra benefit brought by the change in features.

Applications

The word "applications" is a formal term for the ways in which a product is used, and new applications can easily arise even for a product or service that's been around since the dawn of forever.   One good example is the ancient windmill, which has emerged anew as a practical alternative energy source in an era of energy consciousness. In recent times, it had been relegated to primarily decorative roles or occasionally as a wind-driven pump.   More currently, however, it has been attached to electrical generators and storage batteries, a new and newsworthy energy-related application for Don Quixote's one-time opponent.

For your product or service, the contrast in time need not be so drastic.   If you manufacture an electronic test instrument and discover that for the first time the device is being used to service slot machines, this new application warrants a release.   If you are a barber and find that a return to sky-high hemlines is bringing young ladies in for a shave of the legs, this new application for your services warrants a release.

One outstanding example of a new application being newsworthy came about during World War II when the army discovered that anti-freeze in tank radiators elevated the boiling point of the water in them. Barrels of anti-freeze were shipped to army units on desert assignment, and a famous publicity story of the era was born.

But again, the contrasts need not be so drastic for your story.   All you need to do is find a customer who uses your product or service in a novel or interesting way.

There is an obvious opportunity here to use publicity to a tremendous advantage in forging a significant inroad into selling to a new group of customers.   The mechanics are fairly simple.   Once you've identified the new application for your product or service,   make yourself a list of all the different kinds of customers who could use your product or service in this novel way.   Then consult the directories listed in Chapter 3 and prepare a list of these specific publications whose readers include these potential new customers.   Make sure to include these publications on the mailing list for your release.   While you're at it, you should include publications that reach those people who help you sell your product or service (unless, of course, you yourself are the end seller).   If any of these publications offer readers' service inquiry processing, you should soon find yourself with an invaluable list of brand new prospects.

Service

One area where absolutely no change in product or pricing is required but newsworthiness is still possible is the area of service;   we will include warranties and guarantees as part of this subject.

Any time you improve the warranty you offer with a product or service, especially when it makes your warranty protection superior to your competitors' or the standard for your industry, you have reason to share the news through publicity.

One clearcut example of this came to pass in the mid-70s when battery manufacturers began offering lifetime guarantees for their top-of-the-line car batteries.   One thing that didn't make the news is that there was no breakthrough in technology behind the increased protection, just a smart marketing team.

They discovered that the buying habits of American car-buyers at the time showed that buyers rarely kept a car more than 4 years before trading it in on a new one.   Since they had offered 48-month warranties for some time, it was no tough trick to convert these into a lifetime warranty, stipulating that it was good for as long as the buyer owned the car.   As a hedge, consider (as they did) that replacement batteries are rarely purchased for new cars, and most often are required only after the car is 2 or 3 years old.

The result was a lot of publicity and favorable positioning for their batteries, with the implication that technical improvements were at the root of the offering.   Here's one case of a benefit without a feature, which helps illustrate the advantage a benefit holds over a feature every time.

Another significant opportunity is in offering an easier or more convenient way for a customer to solve problems with a product or service.   This could involve longer hours for a service department, telephone advisors, more service personnel, a cooperative arrangement with other dealers or an outside service organization, a consumer affairs staff (as small as one person part-time or as large as you think appropriate), and so on.

Sales

Are sales for any specific product or service you offer up?   Or down? Have you made any large sales recently?   Any of these are reasons for issuing a release.

There's a technique you may want to use in issuing this kind of news: Quote an officer of your own company or, when possible, several significant customers, on his or her personal interpretation of why the particular sales phenomenon is occurring.   This adds credibility to your story and gives an editor the option of including remarks by an "industry spokesperson" in covering (or choosing whether or not to cover) the state of the business.

Non-Changes

As we said at the beginning of this chapter, there are times you can get publicity for your product or service even if none of these factors has changed.

Have your prices remained the same?   In an era hallmarked by spiralling inflation, this in itself is newsworthy, especially if a cost in one area is offset by an economy in another, allowing you to maintain constant pricing.   Here are some ways a release might be headlined to illustrate the newsworthiness of this "non-news":

"Company avoids price increases by absorbing increased cost of materials."

"Prices of (your product or service) still at 19XX (year) levels despite inflation."

"Competition in (your industry) keeps prices low for time being."

"Company announces price freeze at least through (date)."

"Company delays planned price increase until (date) or later; (reason) cited as reason."

Similarly, if there are no changes in the hours, locations, or means by which your product or service is available to your customers, you can spotlight this consistency in a release.   Again, here are some sample headlines to illustrate:

"Company maintains same hours to assure continued availability to customers; cites buyer needs as reason."

"No cutbacks in hours or locations for (company) despite increased operating costs."

"Company avoids adding mail order, cites customer preference for personal contact."

Nothing new about your product at all?   Fine!   That makes it proven and reliable.   Which you can again take advantage of with

FOOD MARKETING INSTITUTE

RESEARCH
EDUCATION
PUBLIC AFFAIRS

1750 K STREET N W
WASHINGTON D C
20006

TEL (202) 452-8444

TELEX 892722 FMI USA WSH

TO: National Press

FROM: Jeffrey R. Prince
Vice President
Communications

SUBJECT: 50th Anniversary Kit

DATE: May 27, 1980

        In the early years of the Depression, food retailers
combined self-service, one-stop shopping and mass merchandising
techniques to create the first supermarkets. This new kind of
food outlet was a unique American invention quickly accepted by
the public and later copied around the world.

        During the next five decades, the supermarket evolved
in response to social changes in the country. Through the post-
war boom, the turmoil of the '60's and the subtle social revolu-
tion of the '70's, its story is inseparable from the demographic
history of the American people.

        This year supermarket firms all over the country are
celebrating the 50th anniversary of the supermarket concept.
Here are some materials which will help you tell the story of
this remarkable retail outlet. The kit includes two press releases, one short and the other a lengthy feature story; two
photographs of early supermarkets; and camera-ready copy of an
ad saluting the industry and the anniversary logo.

        For further information, please contact FMI or local
supermarket operators, who can tell you about the history of
their own firms.

FIFTY YEARS
OF
SUPERMARKETING
1930-1980

Figure 2-1.   News from "olds" can be accomplished on historical anniversaries.
Reproduced here are a cover letter and news release included in a press kit issued by
the Food Marketing Institute on the 50th anniversary of the "supermarket."
(Courtesy Food Marketing Institute)

RESEARCH
EDUCATION
PUBLIC AFFAIRS

FOOD MARKETING INSTITUTE

1750 K STREET, N.W., WASHINGTON, D.C. 20006   TEL. (202) 452-8444   TELEX: 892722 FMI USA WSH

CONTACT: Jeffrey R. Prince
               Vice President
               202/452-8444

50th Anniversary of Supermarket Celebrated

       This year marks the 50th anniversary of the
supermarket, and the event is being celebrated by the
release of a film, the publication of a book and the opening
of a new exhibit at the Smithsonian Institution in Washington. Locally, supermarket firms are planning their own
celebrations.

       During the early years of the Depression, food
retailers combined self-service, one-stop shopping and
mass merchandising techniques to create the first food
outlets that could be called supermarkets. The earliest
examples, frequently referred to as "cheapies," were opened
in empty garages and factories. They had to fight for
survival against established service grocery stores.

       Early supermarkets were well suited to the diffi-
cult Depression years. Stores were undecorated and goods
were piled high on counters and in baskets on the floor.
They often had animal names like Giant Tiger and Great
Leopard, and sensational newspaper ads emphasized the
beast's power to crush prices.

More

Figure 2-1 *(Continued)*

In the decades following the Depression, the super market evolved in response to changing consumer needs. "We have survived because during those 50 years we never lost the ability to change with the times and adapt to customer demand," says Robert O. Aders, President of Food Marketing Institute (FMI), a trade association representing 1175 retail and whole sale companies.

Today, there are 33,600 supermarkets doing a combined $154 billion in sales or 77 percent of all retail grocery sales.

The 50th anniversary celebration has prompted a film entitled The Supermarket: A Great American Invention produced for FMI by Philip Morris Inc., and a 112 page photographic essay entitled Supermarkets: 50 Years of Progress, prepared for FMI by Progressive Grocer Magazine. Both depict the successive transformations of the supermarket from the '30's through the present.

In addition, the Smithsonian Institution is planning an exhibit depicting the history of the supermarket. The exhibit will open in August in the Museum of History and Technology, Washington, D. C.

####

Figure 2-1 *(Continued)*

publicity.   By keeping a product the same, you see, you're avoiding the expense of change "for change's sake."   You're avoiding the "spirit of planned obsolescence that seems to pervade so much of modern life."   And you can always imply that there have been no improvements because the product is already perfect.

One technique to help add newsworthiness to this approach is to survey a number of your customers, asking how they would improve your product or service.   Select the best of their answers (for your purposes) and share them in a release.

The same rationale applies to services.   If there's nothing new, you must already be doing everything right.   Why has there been no change?   You can quote a company officer's opinion or a customer, as in the examples above.   Even better, take a look at your own service statistics.   You may find that there have been so few requirements for service (or an ever-decreasing number, or a never-increasing number or percentage) that there's no need for better service arrangements.

Are sales the same as ever?   Then you can report that sales are steady, that customer demand is steady, and that the popularity of your product or service is as strong as ever.

Even better, think of all the reasons sales might be worse than they are (people have less money to spend, but they're still spending as much as ever on your product, for example) and make your steady sales sound like a victory despite "staggering" odds.

You're probably full of ideas by now for applying these tips to the products or services that your company offers, and ideas are the fuel on which that publicity runs.   Use your imagination and you'll discover lots of reasons for sharing news about your "same old stuff."

It's time now to add a long-overdue word of encouragement about your release's chances of appearing.   It's this: Just as space and time budgets might often work against you, they can also work in your favor.   Editors and producers have space they need to fill; time they need to occupy.   The more interesting the material they can put there, the happier they are to do it.   And what you have to tell them could well be more interesting than some of the other material they find themselves dealing with.

In publicity, the only bad news is no news.

3

Editorial Contact

There's a delightful magazine called *Physics Teacher* that reaches primarily teachers of high school physics courses. At one time, they were on the publicity mailing list of a company that made a number of electronic products that could be useful in teaching physics. This particular company was having little or no success in producing sales to educational institutions, despite a years-long advertising and publicity effort. To add to their frustration, one of their larger competitors was handily achieving better and better results in reaching this important marketplace.

Eventually, in reviewing the file of the publicity that had been run by all magazines, the company's publicity director became aware that this particular magazine was delivering a zero batting average for his releases.

In publicity, the way to respond to a poor batting average with a publication is to call them, ask what's wrong, find out if there's some misunderstanding, and even confirm that the releases are actually arriving.

Lo and behold, the explanation was extremely simple. *Physics Teacher* had no place (at least, at that time) in its format to accommodate publicity: There were no new product pages, no announcement pages, no product roundups. Instead, the editorial content consisted almost entirely of articles by teachers on the things they were doing to help communicate their lesson materials. The editor wasn't sure whether to laugh or scold, but did forward a copy of the magazine to the publicity director.

The happy ending was that the publicity director was also the advertising manager, and the company found *Physics Teacher* to be an effective addition to the roster of publications in which they advertised.

There are a multitude of *faux pas*, sins, and acts of ignorance possible in conducting any publicity program, and no one has ever successfully avoided all of them.   But since there are people at both ends of the publicity channel, reasonable ones, forgiving ones, and, by and large, pleasant ones, you need only an open line of communications to keep things running smoothly.

Still, there are steps you can take (and *should* take) to get your relationship with editors off to a good start.   And the best place to start is at the beginning, with a letter of introduction before you send your first release.   Even if you or your company have been con- ducting a publicity program for some time, a letter of introduction can help signal a "new era of cooperation" between the editors you deal with and your own publicity efforts, no matter how large or small.

The Letter of Introduction

What do you want this letter of introduction to accomplish?   Consider carefully; it can do a lot for you.

First, of course, you'll want to make sure you're reaching the right editor.   If you deal in frozen foods, your releases will never run if they are reaching the editor who handles health and beauty aids.   If you repair typewriters, the editor who only handles cameras and radios has no reason to run your releases.   And no matter what your product or service, you don't want to send your releases to an editor who's retired or moved to another publication.

You'll then want to get the editor's help in identifying everyone who could possibly have an interest in relaying your news, including freelance authors (those who write speculatively or on assignment, then sell specific stories to publications), editors in related   areas (business editors, for example, in addition to news, new product, and feature editors), and so on.

You'll   also want to make sure you tell the people you reach why they will be interested in your particular product or service, and why their readers are likely to be interested.   You don't have to spell everything out for each person, but you do have to give each person some way to ask, "huh?"   Which brings up a fundamental point.

The reason you're preparing this letter of introduction is to open up lines of communication, so make yourself accessible.   Give full name, address, and telephone data on everybody in your organization who will be in direct contact with editors, including extensions, hours they're available (the days of the week and time zones), the TWX or

Telex (teletypewriter) numbers for you at your company, and anything else that will make it easy for an editor to get hold of you or your company.

It's also a good idea to identify what your company does, what your products or services are, who uses them, and why.   Skip the obvious, but don't assume too much.

So much for theory.   Let's get down to one example of a get-acquainted letter you may want to use as a basis for your own:

Dear editor,

If you can spare a minute from your busy day, I hope this letter can help us to make sure we don't take any more of your time than is necessary in the future.

I'm (name), Publicity Director for (company).   We are implementing a new publicity program, and as an important first effort I want to make sure we reach the right editors, authors, and journalists.

We are manufacturers (dealers, distributors, whatever) of (description of product or service).   We have reason to believe that our products (or services) are of interest to your readers.   If you don't agree, please contact me.   I would like to discuss why I believe your readers will be interested in us, or to hear why you believe otherwise.

If you know of other editors, authors, or reporters who would be appropriate for us to reach, we will be delighted to add their names to our mailing list.   Again, a word or a line from you is all that is necessary.   I have enclosed a self-addressed, stamped envelope to make contacting us as easy as possible.

Also, I would like to make myself and my staff available to you for any information you might need about us at any time.   We will be more than happy to cooperate with you and to do what we can to make your job easier.

You can contact me at the address and phone number listed on our letterhead, or talk to   (name) in my absence.   We are available weekdays from 9:00 to 5:00, central time (or as appropriate).

We have a great deal of exciting and interesting news to share.   And you'll be happy to know that we are taking steps to assure that only those news releases which we believe are of interest to your readers will be forwarded to you.

You'll be seeing the first of our new news program very soon. Here's looking forward to a long and friendly association.

Sincerely,

(signature)
(name)
Publicity Director

You will want to juggle terminology somewhat if you include broadcasters in your publicity program. Instead of editors, you will be writing to news directors and producers; instead of readers, you will be referring to listeners, viewers or an audience. But no matter whom you're dealing with, you're dealing with people. And you don't need a course at a charm school to understand that people react well to courtesy and responsiveness.

Using the Phone

Regardless of the size and scope of the publicity program you pursue, it will always be to your advantage to find an opportunity to directly contact at least some of the editors who are important to you. The telephone can be a tremendous ally in any publicity program because it not only helps you make person-to-person contact, it also adds credibility and reality, in a sense, to all the releases you send to that particular editor from that day on. A phone call as a prelude or follow-up to a specific release can not only draw an editor's attention to it, it can also impart a sense of immediacy and urgency. Choose wisely, though. You'll want to be known for good leads, not bum steers.

In calling an editor, always be sure to identify both yourself and the company you're with or the company you're representing. You may also want to identify your publicity role, though it's often implied in your message.   Then state immediately why you're calling:

> "I'm (name) with (company), and I'm calling to alert
> you to our announcement of (release subject), which
> should reach you by (hit date).   I want you to know
> I'm available to you for any additional information you
> might need—now or at any time in the near future.   I
> can give you my name again, if you'd like, and my
> phone number, or you'll find them both on the release."

You've identified yourself, stated your business succinctly, and offered your services as a liaison; now let the editor take it from there. If he or she seems to want to get off the phone quickly, don't worry. There may be a meeting in progress, something urgent demanding immediate attention, or an appointment.   You can always call back or have the editor get back to you later.   Listen carefully for advice and instructions on recontacting.

While most editors and reporters are often busy, they're seldom rude and usually both amicable and cooperative.   They may want to hear the release over the phone.   If there are any questions,   be prepared to respond.   If additional information is needed, do what you can over the phone and promise to put it into writing on whatever schedule is needed.   If you get a   "no thanks,"   you might ask if there's anyone else on staff who might be more interested.   If there's time, you might also ask if there's anything special   he looked for in a story, or if there's anything about this story that prompted a decision against it.   After all, the less you waste each other's time, the more productive your relationship and the easier it will be for both of you.

If the editor or a reporter has asked you for information, be sure to phone that it's on its way.   In fact, it's good practice to call again and make sure it's arrived.   Make extra copies just in case the first one gets lost in transit.

Once editors know that you're "out there," there are times they'll be contacting you.   For example, many magazines and newspapers from time to time will feature an "editorial spotlight" or "editorial focus" wherein they turn their attention to one specific   kind   of product or one specific industry or business.   Routinely, they will send out an   "editorial call," which we'll discuss in more detail in a moment.   This is usually a 1-page form letter that explains what the publication is planning and asks you to provide them with information, either in the form of an open-ended statement or as answers to specific questions.

When responding to an "editorial call"—and you should always respond, even if only to say that company policy precludes answering some or all of the questions—it's a good idea to contact the editor to see if there's anything else you can offer in addition to the requested information.   Earlier releases on the subject, pictures relevant to the subject, product literature, and new quotes from key company management figures are typical of the additional information that most editors welcome in preparing these reports.

Another important way to use the telephone is to find out who you should be talking to at any specific publication.   The switchboard operator is usually very cooperative and very knowledgeable about this, and even if not, always knows who is.   You may end up talking to a lot of different people before you get the answers you need, but it's far better for you to do the running around than for your releases to go on a wild goose chase.

Locating Editors

Of course, before you contact an editor, you need to know where to call or write.   Fortunately, there are dozens of published directories of publicity contacts.   And while you could easily spend thousands of dollars if you were to try to buy or subscribe to all of them, you don't need them all.   Your library (or a large one nearby) probably has several on hand.   And if you are using an advertising or publicity agency, the chances are excellent that they have these references on hand.

Bacon's Publicity Checker lists the trade and specialty press, agricultural and farm journals, consumer magazines, and the business and financial editors of about 700 daily newspapers.   The price is around $50.   It's published by Bacon's Publishing Company, 14 East Jackson Boulevard, Chicago, Illinois 60604 (312-922-8419).

Broadcasting Annual has information on every radio and television station in America, and costs about $30.   It's published by Broadcasting Magazine, 1735 DeSales Street NW, Washington, D. C. 20036 (202-638-1022).

The *Directory of Publications* includes thoroughly cross-indexed information on well over 20,000 newspapers, magazines, trade publications, and college and university publications in the U.S.A., Canada, and elsewhere.   In the $50 price class, it's published by Ayer Press, West Washington Square, Philadelphia, Pennsylvania 19106 (215-829-4000).

Editor & Publisher International Yearbook lists extensive information about every daily newspaper in the U.S.A., Canada, Europe,
and additional countries.   It includes contact information, circulation,
coverage area, key editors and writers, special editions, and more.
The U.S.A. section is organized by state (in alphabetical order), with
cities in the state and papers within the cities also in alphabetical
order.   In the $30 price range, it's published by Editor & Publisher
Company, 575 Lexington Avenue, New York, New York   10022
(212-752-7050).

The *National Radio Publicity Directory* covers radio talk shows,
their audiences, and staff personnel at radio stations across the U.S.A.
This one is in the over-$60 range.   The publisher is Peter Glenn Publica-
tions, Limited, 17 East 48th Street, New York, New York 10017 (212-
688-7940).   Its listings also include network and syndicated talk
shows.

The "bible" of advertising agencies is the *SRDS* series of guides—
formally, the *Standard Rate and Data Service*.   Actually, there are
several volumes published by *SRDS*.   You'll be most interested in
those on business publications, consumer publications, and newspapers,
though there are additional volumes that cover radio and television.
Designed primarily as a source book for information about audience
statistics, advertising costs, and related requirements, these guides also
perform an outstanding job of identifying the specific editorial "slant"
of each publication.   Furthermore, publications are grouped by audience, so you can find the particulars on all the publications reaching
any particular special-interest audience either by looking up the category or by looking up any publication.   (There is a complete by-title
index near the front.)   These categories are very specialized, often
segregating publications that reach manufacturers of a product from
those that reach sellers, from those that reach users, and so on.   The
editorial purpose of each publication is described, key editorial personnel identified, and complete address and telephone information
given.   Costs of the several volumes vary, but may be considered in
general to be among the more expensive (and more thorough) source
books.   Costs include both basic volumes and updates.   These are
published by *Standard Rate and Data Services*, 5201 Old Orchard
Road, Skokie, Illinois 60076 (312-470-3100).

There are three directories published by Oxbridge Publishing Company, Incorporated, 40 East 34th Street, New York, New York 10022
(212-689-8524).   The *Standard Periodical Directory* (over-$60
range) lists magazines, newsletters, directories, and selected local
publications.   The *Standard Directory of Newsletters* ($20 range)
lists—can you guess?—newsletters; thousands of them.   And the

Directory of College Student Press in America (also in the $20 range) lists school papers, yearbooks, literary magazines, and more for about 2,000 schools.

There are also a number of excellent directories available from the National Research Bureau, Incorporated, 424 North Third Street, Burlington, Iowa 52061 (319-752-5415). *Working Press of the Nation* offers several volumes covering different types of media: newspapers, magazines, radio, television, feature writers, and syndicates. The set is in the over-$150 bracket. *Gebbie House Magazine Directory* (over-$35 bracket) covers more than 4,000 "house" publications— a category which includes everything from company newsletters to company magazines and journals. Audiences of these include employees, customers, or investors, depending on the specific publication. *Gebbie Press All-In-One Directory*, in the $50 range, offers the addresses of daily and weekly newspapers, TV and radio broadcasting stations, and magazines in the consumer, farm, trade, and business press categories in the U.S.A.

If you are considering a strictly local publicity effort, reaching only people in your own community or area, don't overlook the telephone directory. While your local *Yellow Pages* may not contain all these categories, here are some that should start you on your way:

> News publications—trade, association, etc.
>
> News services
>
> Newspaper feature syndicates
>
> Newspapers
>
> Publishers—directory and guide
>
> Publishers—periodicals (magazines)
>
> Radio program producers
>
> Radio stations and broadcasting companies
>
> Television—CATV companies (cable TV)
>
> Television program producers
>
> Television stations and broadcasting companies

Publicity and Press Relations

Recently, a marketing executive at one of America's largest companies described publicity as getting his company's name out to the public as often and as favorably as possible.   Publicity is certainly capable of accomplishing this, but there's another aspect of marketing communications that can help make any program more effective: *press relations.*

About the simplest possible definition of press relations is full cooperation with editors, producers, news directors, authors, reporters, and journalists.   Sometimes this can mean acting as their "gopher" or informal assistant.   Often this means responding to editorial calls with special articles, explanations, opinions, or photography. It may also mean providing a company spokesman for a panel discussion, talk show, or interview.

But the term is even easier to understand if, instead of trying to describe what press relations means, we look at what press relations can accomplish.   And for that, we ought to put ourselves in an editor's chair, at least for a brief mental exercise.

An editor's job is to fill the pages of a publication, or at least those assigned to that particular editor, with the most current, most relevant, most interesting, and most newsworthy information a reader could hope to find; one pertinent to the topic and point of view of the editor's assigned "beat."   There are only a limited number of tools and resources available to help accomplish this task.

One of these is publicity; but only one of several.   While there are any number of publications in which product news releases and other publicity-generated news represent the overwhelming majority of editorial material, these are only one class of publication, and they do not offer the same credibility and apparent objectivity that can be realized through third-party coverage of your company's products or services.

By third-party coverage we mean prepared articles, reviews, and reports that reflect more than a simple pick-up, editing, or rewrite of news releases.   Most publications depend more on this type of coverage than any other.

That's one reason it's a good idea to include freelance authors on your publicity mailing list: They're the people who often prepare these articles, reviews, and reports, and the more they know about you, your products, your services, and your activities, the better the chance you'll be included to your best advantage when they prepare their materials.   Conversely, if they've never heard of you or don't realize that you're active in the specific area for which they're preparing materials, you stand a small chance of being included to your best advantage, if at all.   Also, there's the simple human factor of expedience and convenience to consider.   If an author or reporter suspects you may be active in that particular area and one of your recent releases is "coincidentally" at hand, your phone number is that much more available, and your chance of being contacted that much stronger. Contact your key editors for the names of prominent freelancers.

What's true for freelancers, of course, is true for staff reporters at those organizations large enough to have someone other than the editor on staff.   Here, though, you can assume that as long as the editor has your releases available, they'll be packaged with other background materials and handed to the reporter with the assignment.

Incidentally, you can count on most of your releases not being filed at the publication, so don't be surprised if you get a call asking for another copy.   Always print between 5 and 20% more releases than you immediately need for mailing, and keep them in a backfile for just such requests.

Which brings us back to the editor's chair and another important resource, the *editorial call*.   This is a request for information that uses the publicity channel in reverse, with editors contacting those people and organizations of which they're aware and asking for specific kinds of information.

Editorial calls vary from publication to publication, but there are a few basic kinds.   One is very open-ended, and will read something like this:

> We are planning a special report on (subject) and would like to invite you to participate.   Please send us any pertinent information, including press releases, catalog sheets, and brochures.   Also, please include appropriate black-and-white glossy photographs. Enclose your current pricing, and any other information you feel will help us provide the best possible coverage of this subject.

Another kind is much more specific.   Essentially a questionnaire, it will ask for specifics about your products or services, and may also ask for company statements on what you believe to be significant trends or developments in the field, what you see coming in the future, what users or customers are demanding, the state of the art, any changes in the marketplace, any changes in the way you sell the product, and so on.

It is always in your best interests to reply as quickly and completely as company policy permits.   If company policy prohibits answering any specific questions, say so, and try to explain why.   For example:

> We consider (subject) to be proprietary information, and respectfully decline to provide specific answers

to this question.   If you could rephrase the question in less specific terms, perhaps we could provide more helpful information.

Even when an editorial call asks for specific information only, feel free to include any comments or information you feel it is in your best interest to see in print.   The editor may think this "bonus" information is a worthwhile addition to the planned coverage, providing a more complete picture of the subject.   Or perhaps you may prompt a later feature on the topic you suggest.

One variation of the editorial call is the *call for articles*, which is a publication's way of providing an up-to-date picture of the trends and developments inside various companies active in a given industry. The call for articles is an invitation to let someone within your company write the requested article.   Many times, this will be a "how" article, describing how your company approaches a specific task or problem, or an "applications" article, describing how your products or services are being used.   And many times, it will be ghost written by a publicity writer, using information from the "expert."

Often, there's an informal understanding that publications reaching special interest audiences are open to articles from within each special interest area, even without a formal call for articles being issued.   Feel free to contact someone within your organization capable of preparing an article.   Then, before you actually set those wheels in motion, contact one selected editor (choose the publication you think most likely to carry this type of article to the audience you want most, and shop carefully).   Question his or her interest in the article you select. Editors usually welcome this interest, and are very helpful in providing advice on how to slant the article for that publication's readers.   For example, some publications prefer seeing a bigwig's byline—no matter who actually did the writing.

Many publications have prepared very helpful   "author's guide" materials. Ask for them.

Professionals know that a query does not necessarily guarantee that an article will run, and editors always retain the right of revision, but this procedure is the one they follow to help improve the chances that everything will go smoothly.

By the way, this is also an excellent method of developing a closer association, higher regard, more personal relationship, and occasionally, even friendship with editors.   And that, after all, is the ultimate goal of press relations.

Remember, the editor has a job to do, and the more you can make it part of your job to help him or her do it, the better the results for your company.

FOOD MARKETING INSTITUTE

1750 K STREET N.W. WASHINGTON D.C. 20006   TEL (202) 452-8444   TELEX 892722 FMI USA WSH

June 16, 1980

** NEWS ADVISORY **

The Food Marketing Institute recently presented its recommendations to the Republican and Democratic Platform Committees concerning vital issues to the food retail and wholesale industry, as well as the American consumer. Our hope is that both parties will encorporate appropriate language into their platforms since we believe our suggestions to be essential to the welfare of the nation's food distribution system.

We believe these suggestions will be of interest to you. If you have any questions, please feel free to contact us.

```
Contact:  Jack Cergol           Jeffrey R. Prince
          Manager        or     Vice President
          Communications        Communications

               (202) 452-8444
```

Figure 3-1.   The reverse of an editorial call is a "news advisory," which alerts the editor that a story is available without giving details, requiring that the editor contact you. (Courtesy Food Marketing Institute)

Early Warnings and Replies

Your competitors are probably just as interested in good publicity and good press relations as you are, and may be even more aggressive in pursuing these goals.   Within your industry, there may be strong lines of partisanship that divide camps, making competitors "the enemy." Few editors can afford to take sides in these unofficial battles, and most will make an effort to assure that they present balanced coverage.

So once an editor gets to know you, chances are you'll hear about some of the things your competitors are up to from time to time. If there's an article by one of them on a topic, you may be invited to present an article from another viewpoint.   If a particularly strong opinion is being presented, in a letter to the editor, for example, you may be invited to reply.   If they're presenting one way to solve a problem, you may be invited to present another.

Editors generally would rather leave decisions about who's better or worse, who's right or wrong, to the reader.   And even when you aren't given a head-to-head opportunity to present your side of the story, you'll rarely be excluded from replying (since this could lead to potential legal difficulties), and you'll often have at least an early warning of what's about to be presented.

It's all part of establishing good editorial contacts.   You must learn whom to talk to where, and about what. Do your best to get to know the people on the other side of the channel, what their needs are, and how you can help. And do your best to cooperate.

The Phone Vs. the Mail

Most editors most of the time would prefer that you let your fingers do their walking across a typewriter instead of a telephone. Nevertheless, there are times when only a phone call will get the job done, and it's a rare editor who won't take calls.   But unless the call asks for information that can be conveyed in a few words, or conveys information that can't wait for the mail, most calls are an unnecessary step for you and a bother for editors: And the editor is going to ask you to put it in writing and send it in anyway.

So when do you use the mail? When do you call? Both are appropriate under certain circumstances; both are important in the overall maintenance of good editorial contact.   So let's take a look at which to use when, and why.

The Editor's Desk

Editors usually pride themselves on keeping current with all the latest developments in their fields.   It's a nearly inescapable feeling when so much current information is focused at their desks day in and day out. And since the great majority of editors take their responsibility to keep current very seriously, most read every release and every scrap of news that comes is.

But not every word.   There simply isn't time for that.

Every piece of mail is opened, and often stamped with the date it's received.   Most envelopes are immediately discarded, which is why it's important to include complete address and contact information on the release or letterhead itself.

Then the day's   "big read" begins, usually as an accompaniment to the morning coffee.

Press releases are particularly identifiable, since most are either printed on distinctive news release letterhead or are prominently marked   "For immediate release," "Press information," or similarly distinguished from correspondence.

The stack of daily mail on a typical editor's desk will vary from a few inches to several feet thick—each day!   And while most editors are secretly jealous of Evelyn Wood, only a few percent have been formally trained in speed reading.

As a result, the first cursory judgment on the fate of most releases is based on a quick reading of the headline and a paragraph or two. In Chapter 3, we've already discussed how to give a release its best chance of running.   We know that not every release contains earth-shattering news, and many are designed specifically for the purpose of keeping the company's name in front of the public.   So, for most releases, taking a chance on having a release picked up is justified; in the long run, enough will be run in enough places to justify the overall effort.

But there will be times when some bit of information will be especially newsworthy, timely, urgent, or significant to at least one editor at one publication.   That's the time to pick up the phone—unless it happens to be the "busy time" of the editor's day, week, or month. As you learn of these busy times, jot down a note of them next to the editor's phone number in your index.

Editors, as we've seen, are particularly sensitive to significant announcements, and no more want to miss them than you would want to have them missed.   So it's perfectly proper for you to call and bring your news to the editor's attention.

The best time to do this is the day after you mail the release. (For these especially significant announcements, you may want to consider using the office copier to get the word to a selected few publications more quickly than is possible with the usual print-stuff-and-mail procedure.)

When you call, keep the message brief unless the editor wants more specifics.   Announce who you are and identify your company; then the conversation should go something like this:

> We sent you a press release in yesterday's mail an-
> nouncing (the subject of the release). This is important
> to us and we think it's something you'll definitely want
> to pass on to your readers. It should reach you in a day
> or two, and I hope you'll be able to flag it when it
> arrives.   Give me a call if you need more information.
> You'll find my name and number on the release.   If
> there's anything else I can tell you now, please ask.

Now the editor knows that the release is coming, that it merits more than the usual attention, and whom to contact for more information.

A Bad Example

The procedure above is the right way to use the phone in conjunction with an important publicity release, but there are any number of wrong ways. If you learn to recognize them—and why they're not the best way to do business—you'll have a much better grasp on how not to waste time and trouble on either side of the channel.

One wrong move would be to try to call the editor with your news and relay it over the phone.   First, it's very demanding on an editor's time.   Second, it's terribly presumptuous.   Third, even if you do talk an editor into taking your dictation (that's what it amounts to) you'll inevitably cause some resentment.   Unless the editor has called you to ask for information over the phone, put the printed words into the mail or courier service, or send them by wire.

Another wrong move would be to call the editor before you're prepared to send your information.   Most editors will insist on some-thing in writing, and if what you have to say is so terribly important, why isn't it worth your time to prepare it?   Isn't the editor's time important to you?   Or are you trying to pull the wool over somebody's eyes by crying "wolf" when there is none?   Your credibility is tre-mendously important to your publicity function, and once lost, terribly hard to re-establish.

Nor should you insist that the editor run your release.   You can urge, you can plead your case, you can ask and you can explain, but the decision has to be the editor's.   It isn't so much a case of putting yourself at the editor's mercy as it is a case of trusting the editor's judgment. If what you have to share is as significant and newsworthy as you think, your news will make it on its own merits;   instead of aggravating the editor, you'll be doing both the editor and the publication a service by helping them keep on top of the news.

And if you wait too long before you call, there's a good chance the release has already been processed.   If it got rejected, no editor is going to go fishing through the wastebasket trying to find it; you'll only have to send another copy, and the extra delay could mean missing a deadline, which means waiting as long as 2 to 3 months before your news appears.   If it's been accepted, the editor may or may not remember, and probably won't want to go to the trouble of chasing it down;   consider that your release could have gone out for typesetting, be on another floor, or off the premises entirely.   So, again, avoid the problem by calling before the release arrives.

Any Questions?

There are going to be times when you're preparing a release or answering an editorial call and you won't be sure of how to handle something. If you can condense your confusion down to a few simple questions, most editors are more than willing to lend a hand with a bit of advice or at least an opinion.

One excellent guideline is to write the question down and stare at it for a while.   If you would be embarrassed to ask the question in a letter, the chances are you shouldn't ask it over the phone either.

Most of the questions you'll have will involve clarification of your understanding of something.   What does a particular question on an editorial call mean?   Can the editor rephrase it to help you understand how to relate it to your products or services?   Can the editor venture a guess as to what your answer might be to help you give a more complete answer?

Or the questions you have may involve interpreting one of your announcements in a way that will help it to make more sense to a particular editor's audience.   Don't ask the editor to write your release for you, but it's okay to ask for personal advice on the best way to write it.   The editor can probably give you some valuable insight into the problems most readers of the publication are facing, and perhaps lead you to a better understanding of how what you offer can help them.

But should you call or should you write?

In this case, you should call, since a call will involve less of an editor's time than a letter, and since you're likely to need a reply sooner than the mails would permit.   But it's important not to take too much of an editor's time on the phone, either.   There's an easy way to make sure you don't.

Take some time yourself.   Make a list of questions and put it away for about an hour.   Then read the questions again: Do they still make sense?   Can you simplify them?   Make them easier to answer?   Once you're satisfied that you've simplified your questions as much as possible, organize yourself and make the call.   You'll gain a reputation as a professional who knows how to ask the right questions and who doesn't waste an editor's time.

Channeling Anger

There may be a time that you'll want to pick up the phone and do yourself no good at all.   This is when you read something that makes you angry; misrepresentation of you, your company, or your products or services, an unfavorable comment or attitude, or a sin of omission.

Don't do it.

The editor may not have realized that something was likely to raise your ire.   If it's an oversight, most editors will bend over backward to set things right.   Even if the editor is involved in a little rabble rousing at your expense, there's no fight without a second contestant, and the wrong kind of reply can make you look very much like the villain.

Here's how to respond when somebody does you damage.

First, decide exactly what it is that's wrong or unfair.   Is there a misquote?   A quote taken badly out of context?   A misinterpretation? A vicious statement?   Is the publication citing something about your company that isn't true?   Something that was once true but has since been corrected?   Underline those passages you think are most damaging, sit down, and start working on the first of many drafts for a letter you may or may not send.

Do not put into writing that you are upset or angry; rather, point out that you either disagree with what was said or that you believe the editor wasn't entirely aware of all the pertinent facts.   Cite the pertinent passages and give your side of the story.   Invite the editor to contact you directly for more information.   And don't have it typed.

The next day, have another look at the letter.   If the editor were to reprint it in its entirety, would it show you and your company in the best possible light?   Does it make you look petty?   Vengeful?   Unsporting? And what if the editor were to edit the letter down to excerpts? Do the parts stand the same test as the whole? If not, rewrite, and try the same test again after waiting another day.

Once you're satisfied that the letter properly and appropriately represents you, mail it. Two or three days later—or longer—ask the editor whether the letter's arrived. If it hasn't, ask the editor to please contact you once it does. If it has, the editor will probably either open the conversation or refuse to talk to you.

If the editor is willing to talk to you at all, it's a good sign. Be calm, reserved, friendly, and patient, and give the editor every opportunity to offer some solution. If the editor is belligerent, get off the phone as quickly and as graciously as possible. Your options at that point include taking it up with his publisher, taking it up with competing editors, or taking it up with your attorneys.

One instance we haven't mentioned is that the coverage is absolutely true and accurate and that you've been caught red-handed doing something to make you unpopular with a given audience. If you think it's possible to explain your actions or attitudes in such a way that they seem more reasonable (and less villainous) to that audience, carefully plan and execute a statement of your position and contact the editor by mail about running it, with a confirming phone call.

Another option is to plead ignorance; that you didn't realize that what you were caught at would have such an effect. Apologize, and announce whatever reasonable corrective measures you will take. Then document them and share that with the editor in question.

Another option is to lie low for a while and wait for the whole thing to blow over. This won't do you any good, but it may at least do you less harm than being too visible at the wrong time. And while you're in hiding, it's a good idea to consult your business advisors or attorneys.

Now that the unpleasant business is out of the way—and here's hoping you never need those last bits of advice—let's summarize the principles in deciding when to write and when to use the phone.

- If it would take 30 seconds to a minute to communicate what you have to say, put it in writing.

- If the wording of what you have to say is important, put it in writing.

- If important facts or specifications are significant to what you have to say, put it in writing.

- If it isn't urgent, put it in writing.

- If it's going to take the editor some time to prepare an answer, put it in writing.

- If it's brief, urgent, newsworthy, requires an interactive conversation, and is important to the editor's audience— or any 3 of these 5 considerations is true—call.

4

Meeting the Press

Like anyone who's ever corresponded with a pen pal for any length of time, you're going to develop a certain respect, friendship, camaraderie, and even curiosity about the editors you work with. Even if there's no pressing reason, you'll probably find some way of getting together with as many editors as you can. The chances are that the first time you'll see many of these people is when you finally have a big announcement to make, and you've decided to make the investment in a press conference or media event.

There are two separate phenomena in that last paragraph; meeting editors just to meet them, and meeting editors for the purpose of handing out a story. Both are valid, and both can be done professionally, but each corresponds to a different circumstance. Let me share a story I heard over the phone just yesterday.

An editor friend was chatting with me about this very chapter. I asked what prompted him to decide whether or not to attend a press conference or similar function. He answered that the likelihood of the announcement being of interest to his readers is the first concern, and the chances of it doing the magazine some good—developing a rapport that could lead to advertising, for example—the second concern. And then he told me about a very surprising function that he had attended. It was hosted by Motorola, for members of their "Technical Press Club," an unofficial organization made up of the editors they invited to attend.

The most remarkable and memorable aspect of this "Technical Press Club" in the minds of the editors I talked to is that despite being a lavish cocktail party, complete with gift mugs to take home, there was no "pitch," no attempt to try to "sell" them a story.

The man responsible for this brainchild is the man in charge of Motorola's public relations, Lothar Stern. Lothar explains, "This is our way of saying thanks for your cooperation, for working with us, and for permitting us to work with you." Lothar's office is with Motorola's group headquarters in Phoenix, which is off the "route" for most of the technical press in Boston, New York, and New Jersey; as a result, only a few editors are able to visit Phoenix for face-to-face meetings. With the receptions given for the "Technical Press Club," Lothar and his staff had an opportunity to meet a great many more editors face to face and build rapport. Most of these receptions are timed to coincide with major trade shows, so many editors are already on hand, making the party easy to get to.

Just thought you'd be interested in how one of the top professionals looks at this opportunity. Your operation may be nowhere near the size and sophistication of the one run by Motorola, but there's no reason for you to adopt a less classy attitude toward your relations with the press.

There's another side to this picture, too; a bleaker side. It leaves a bad taste in the minds of editors toward "those publicity guys," and it's all due to a few people who don't do their homework. It's a function—press conference, press party, press breakfast—where either the "big announcement" is meaningless, or it has absolutely nothing to do with the editor being contacted or that editor's readership. It's called a waste of time, and its side effects go beyond the brief non-encounter.

One editor listed what qualifies these media nonevents as a waste of time:

- The news is already out, so the announcement is anticli-mactic.

- The news has nothing whatsoever to do with the readers of this publication.

- The news is a report of something that isn't newsworthy, like "our progress on the new plant is continuing as expected."

- The news would only merit an inch or two of space and would have been better communicated by a press release.

So how do you avoid wasting an editor's time? How do you prepare an event that editors will consider meaningful or productive? How do you get editors to attend? How can you be sure you're asking the right editors? What do editors expect of you at these functions? How do you plan for results?

For that matter, what goes into setting up a function?   Do you need to put on a lavish "feed" or open a bar?   How do you book a room? Where do you hold the event?   What do you do?   What don't you do? Shall we begin?

Types of Media Events

Remember what we said about media events in Chapter 2: A media event is any presentation you make to a live audience.   The primary intention is to provide material of interest to the news media, who are for the purposes of the media event, the most significant part of that audience.   These events are designed to serve the needs of the news media by providing the urgency, information, interest, and pictorial impact that help any story merit news coverage.

Any function you plan where the attendance of the media is a planned and desired end can be classified as a "media event."   The most common examples of media events are press conferences, press parties or receptions, and a third category which is itself often called "media event" (we'll clear the confusion in a second).   For convenience, you might think of it as a "special event" or as grandstanding.

The first example, the press conference, is a strictly business affair where a spokesperson for your company, an officer, principal, or perhaps yourself, makes a major, significant announcement of importance to the attending representatives of the press and provides them with an opportunity to ask questions and get answers.   Normally, the questions are asked in a formal atmosphere where any member of the press can ask any questions and all will hear the answer.   Also, arrangements can be made for individual question-and-answer sessions or interviews after the formal presentation breaks up.   Press conferences are seldom the site of a lavish feed, though coffee and pastry would be appropriate as a convenience to the attending press representatives.   A special package of press releases, called either a *release package* or a *press kit*, is usually distributed at these events, and there is often someone on hand who can fulfill requests for additional information quickly.

Press parties are similar, but involve a meal, a cocktail party, or both. These functions combine business and pleasure, with a bar or buffet opening before the announced time of the "official statement" or "official announcement," then reopening afterwards.   Press parties (sometimes called "press preview parties") are occasions when significant new products are unveiled to the media.   These products are previewed far enough in advance of their public availability to let the media "show and tell" the products before most people would have a chance to see them.   Press parties are usually afternoon or evening sessions, and invitations may or may not include spouses or guests. The formal question-and-answer period is generally briefer than at a more formal press conference, but with extended opportunities to mingle and corner key individuals for specific interviews or answers during the socializing.   These people should, of course, be briefed on what information can and cannot be divulged.

Press breakfasts, press lunches, and press dinners are a special category of press parties.   Here, the atmosphere is slightly less social and more formal.   The members of the press are generally invited to pick up a drink (which may be non-alcoholic, at your option, like juice, coffee, or tea at a breakfast) and find themselves a place to sit.   The meal is then served and, while they dine, a formal presentation of the announcements prompting the event is made at the head table or head of the room.   These press functions are designed to last a controlled length of time; generally an hour to an hour and a half, possibly two hours for a big dinner and a big announcement.   This permits the members of the press to plan their days and to allow other activities to follow at known times.   On these occasions, you should serve food because you are taking the guests away from their normal meal times, not because you're being especially gracious or hospitable.

The third type of media event has been called "media event." This is mostly because nobody can think of a kinder name, and most shun its earlier name, "publicity stunt," for obvious reasons.   (Thirty, forty, and fifty years ago, these were also called flak-fests, because publicity people were themselves called "flaks," a term derived from the clutter dropped from airplanes to confuse radar and, earlier, ground observers.)   Call them what you will, these activities are planned and executed with the press in mind, regardless of the merit or lack of merit they deserve in a more general context.   We'll discuss this category of activities more thoroughly before the end of this chapter.

Deciding on an Event

You could conceivably conduct a successful publicity program forever without once hosting any kind of press conference, press party, press breakfast, lunch, or dinner or conducting any manner of media event. Indeed, it would be much less expensive for you to shun these activities entirely.   But, obviously, organizations are finding reasons all the time for hosting media events.   Why do they do it?

The first thing we should consider is that you don't have to go to the Plaza Hotel on Central Park in Manhattan, host a gala event to which thousands of the editorial who's-who has been invited, and follow up with diamond brooches for each guest. A simple conference room at a local motel for local media people is more than suitable, and a table with simple refreshments (like coffee and tea) is both fitting and inexpensive. If there are ten or twenty people you would expect to attend, one of the smaller conference rooms should be more than adequate, or you may have a place in your office complex (a conference room or briefing room) that will be adequate; gifts are never required.

Regardless of the size or scope of your activity, someone (probably you) has to make the decision of whether or not to go through the trouble and expense of planning and executing the event. Here are some guidelines to help you decide.

IS THIS MORE NEWSWORTHY THAN USUAL? Unless you're with a major corporation (Fortune 500 size) or hiring a person who is newsworthy independent of your organization (a former President or King, for example), personnel announcements, even for the highest positions in your company, won't warrant much more than a passing reference from the press in any case. New plants and new programs for employees are likely to make a difference only within the specific geographic locations where a large number of people are involved, so only local media would be involved in an event. Are there enough local media people to warrant an effort beyond a release? However, if you can announce a technical or scientific breakthrough or a truly significant new product or service, there may well be reason to consider doing so at a special "unveiling" or "preview" event. Also, if you're producing the "one millionth" doodad on your assembly line, it's okay to invite the press to the "landmark" event. While we've been preaching in previous chapters that anything can be made newsworthy, before you go ahead with an event, make sure your news is not only naturally newsworthy, but even more newsworthy than usual.

CAN YOU OFFER SOMETHING IN PERSON THAT YOU CAN'T OFFER IN A RELEASE? In other words, is there some reason the editor's understanding or appreciation of your announcement will be enhanced through a direct meeting? If seeing something work makes a difference, if seeing what something looks like in "real life" makes a difference, if a chance to work with something in a "hands-on," try-it-yourself situation makes a difference, or if the opportunity to chat with company experts or key people makes a difference, hosting an event may bring the quality and quantity of coverage you want. Once again, brief and prepare your people, anticipate the hard questions, and rehearse your responses.

IS THERE AN EVENTUAL RETURN ON YOUR INVESTMENT?
Planning and executing one of these activities takes a lot of time and
costs a significant amount of money.   Good business practice dictates
that this expenditure should eventually lead to some favorable result,
preferably one that can be measured in the same way as the expenditure: in money.   Will the additional coverage and attention result
in a quicker, more thorough exposure that will yield greater customer
interest, and eventually a greater share of the market for your company's sales?   Will this exposure result in direct orders?   Will it result
in activity for your company's investors?   What return can you expect?
How big?   How soon?   Is it worth it?   When you're considering all
this, decide what the difference in return will be (either amount or time)
by conducting a special activity instead of your usual release program,
and compare that to the extra cost of the special activity.   If you have
any doubts, don't plan the event.

CAN YOU AFFORD IT?   Even when the return on investment is
very attractive, the immediate cash outlay comes up front, and if it's
going to mean a financial hardship, you should opt against planning
the event.

IS IT REASONABLE FOR THE PRESS TO GET TO YOU?   The
specific place and time for which you plan your event will always
eliminate some members of the press from being able to attend.
Carefully review the list of media people you would want to invite
to whatever activity you're considering.   Where are most of them
located?   Is there another event scheduled for the time you're planning yours?   A call to a friendly editor can help find out who else is
"on the dockets."   Is there something happening that will make this
an especially busy time for editors?   The week before a trade show
they plan to attend will be unusually busy because they'll be trying
to work ahead;   the week after even worse because they'll be trying
to catch up.   While many publications afford their editors and writers
a travel allowance, it's often limited and usually saved for *very* special
occasions—is yours one of them, or not quite?   If too many limiting
factors start stacking up against you, it's time to either rethink or give
up on your planned event.

CAN YOU GET EVERYTHING PREPARED IN TIME?   One of the
hardest things about the publicity task to adjust to is that while everything we do carries a feeling of urgency (RUSH!   URGENT!   FOR
IMMEDIATE RELEASE!), we can't always rush from our knowledge
of a news story to our dissemination of it.   This is especially true when
extra planning and preparation are necessary, as with a media event.   In

addition to preparing copy for release, photo sessions, repros of every-thing, extra printed materials like jackets and handling the mailing, and maintenance of invitations, you'll have rooms to book, samples to arrange for, and more things than are ever possible to do within the short time left.   How much time is left?   During that time, how much of your time is available?   And how much time will you need? If the answers don't fit with each other, raise a storm warning flag or call the whole thing off.

If you've passed these preliminary (but crucial) tests successfully, it's time to think about what form your announcement should take. You'll have the best control over the simplest event—a press conference. But if you are addressing a broad variety of publications, be careful lest the question-and-answer repartee at any one time tends not to be of interest to the majority of your audience.   Still, there's no reason not to offer individual question-and-answer periods afterwards,   and   the press conference—because of the things you *don't* have to worry about, like food and drinks and advanced protocol—is the best option for the relative newcomer.   Get a few of these (at least) under your belt before trying to move up to the cafe set.

But circumstances may dictate that meal time is the only time avail-able for your session.   The press breakfast, brunch, luncheon, or dinner is your next best bet.   While there's no reason to lavish caviar and *cordon bleu*   cookery on your assembled guests, neither do you want them leaving with (no pun intended) a bad taste in their mouths due to an unpalatable or simply edible meal.   Regardless (almost)   of the quality of the announcement you make, cardboard roast beast,   un-chewable chicken, or fettuccini awful can ruin your reputation as far as these fetes are concerned, making it terribly hard to draw much of a crowd for your next shindig.   The best advice is to know the esta-blishment you're planning to hold the event in, go there before you book, and ask to actually see (or even taste) the proposed meals.   Lack-ing that, get the name of the last company that hosted a similar event there and the person who handled the arrangements, call, and ask. Don't be bashful—this is how the pros often double check   facility arrangements.

If circumstances force you into a full-blown press party and you've never been involved with that kind of function before, consult with a local home economist (you should be able to find one through a local college, high school, or newspaper) or a caterer with   an   excellent reputation, and use them as paid consultants in making the necessary arrangements.   The few extra dollars you spend may buy you out of grief that you'd later pay ten times the amount to forego.

Making Arrangements

We've gone over some arrangements already, but let's make ourselves a checklist of what you have to do in order to pull everything off.

At Your Company

1.   Decide whether or not it's feasible.

2.   Commit personnel and financial resources.

3.   Arrange for product samples.

4.   Arrange for demonstrations.

5.   Arrange for press release copywriting.

6.   Arrange for photography.

7.   Arrange for printing of press kit jackets.

8.   Arrange to reproduce, collate, and package press kits.

9.   Arrange for availability of collateral materials.

10.   Arrange for key and support personnel.

11.   Arrange for transportation of material.

12.   Arrange for transportation and accommodations (including travel expenses) for personnel, as required.

13.   Send and follow up invitations and confirmations to all media.

14.   Arrange for attendee gifts, if any.

With the Facility

1.   Contact meetings and catering managers.

2.   Compare planned attendance with available facility room sizes.

3.   Select room.

4.   Arrange with facility to provide food and drink service —catering, bartending, etc.

5. Make credit or payment arrangements.

6. Arrange for required audio-visual services.

   a) projectors, stands, screens, power.

   b) microphone, public address, rostrum.

   c) control of room lighting.

   d) back-up equipment, bulbs, etc.

7. Make specific selections of the menu you will provide —hot vs. cold hors d'oeuvres, for example, or *pâte* vs. ribs.

8. Arrange for lobby signboards.

9. Arrange for before/after hospitality suites, if desired.

10. Double check fire safety arrangements.

11. Double check insurance and liability arrangements.

12. Check on accessibility for handicapped.

13. Check on security arrangements to safeguard your material when you're not there; control unwanted visitors when you are.

14. Double check with local police on the character of the hotel and its surroundings.

15. Check on other concurrent functions (noisy groups or raucous parties in the next room or on the way to yours).

16. Get a signed document detailing what they will provide and what you must do in return.

17. Arrange for either cafe style (a large number of small tables, each seating only a few persons), banquet style (a few long tables that seat a great many people), or auditorium style (rows of chairs) seating, whichever is most appropriate for your presentation.

18. Arrange for sufficient ash trays and matches.

19. Learn the names of the key facility people on duty:

    a) Bell captain.

    b) Head of security.

    c)   Banquet manager.

    d)   Meetings manager.

    e)   Custodian.

    f)   Maintenance superintendent.

20.   Arrange for sufficient telephones. (Editors don't mind using pay phones if enough are available, but you may want to have some extra phones installed in or near the meeting room.)

21.   Make arrangements for whatever special services you need, or find out whom to contact:

    a)   Musicians.

    b)   Models.

    c)   Photographers.

    d)   Audio-visual.

    e)   Film or tape camera/sound crews.

    f)   Guards.

22.   Make arrangements for any special handling of your material, like freight handling, special ramps or elevators, special power sources, or electrical tie-ins, etc.

With Local Resources

1.   Contact caterers or a home economist as consultants, if appropriate.

2.   Contact a promotional premium (also called *advertising specialty*) sales organization at least 8 weeks in advance to arrange for custom imprinted gifts, if appropriate.

3.   Have audio-visual materials prepared or produced, as appropriate.

4.   Contact a travel agent for travel plans and news of any pending travel-related labor actions that could make travel for you or the press difficult.

5.   Contact fashion consultants on wardrobe for key personnel to assure crisp, professional appearance.

6. Contact a local signmaker for any required supporting graphics.

After the Event

1. Send thank you letters to attending editors and press.

2. Send thank you letters to key people at the facility. (By the way, it's a good idea to tip them, as appropriate, both before and after they get involved.)

3. Send releases in press kit to all non-attending editors with a "sorry we missed you" cover letter.

4. Fulfill any promises made for additional materials to the press.

5. Issue an additional release on the event with photos taken there.

6. Critique every step of the "operation" carefully and make notes for next time.   (Do this in conference with everyone who attended, if possible.)

7. Send thank you notes, or better, to the key people at your company who helped make the thing come off— especially including those who worked hard but didn't get a chance to go.

8. Pay the bills on time.

Publicity Stunts

A word of caution: "Publicity stunts" is a more memorable subhead than "media events"—but it's a *faux pas* to use this term in public. Perhaps "special events" would be nicer.

In the old days (ouch—I could feel a crop of white whiskers bristling up with that phrase!) "publicity stunts" usually referred to wild schemes designed to get headlines. It might mean faking the kidnapping of a starlet, a bomb threat on a movie lot, announcing a no-chance candidate for a political office (to destroy the *opposing* party's credibility), or announcing a bizarre invention (that never did and never would work).

These days, "special events" are more professional, and often support the best interests of the community as a whole. It might be a company-sponsored camp for underprivileged children, company-sponsored participation in a special charity fund-raising event, or a company-sponsored scholarship or contest.

Or it might be for fun; a lobster race for a seafood restaurant, a Mr. Macho beauty contest for a tux shop, a celebrity lookalike contest for a theater or camera shop, or a quick-draw showdown for an art supply store.

These special events can be on a national level, too. Pillsbury's Bake-Off, Purina's Cat Chow Calendar Cat Contest, and the Colgate/Dinah Shore Golf Classic are good examples of events with strong sponsor tie-ins that generate an uncommonly large volume of publicity. Similarly, the same kind of thing is true every time Goodyear flies its blimps on national television or into any location in the nation.

Let's assume that most of you will be dealing with this type of event more often on a more local level and concentrate on how to accomplish everything you set out to do.   If and when you do find yourself working on a larger scale, you'll find the same principles apply.

But what is it you are setting off to do?   Is publicity the main product or a byproduct?

Don't be noble; publicity *is* the main product.   Any good works you can accomplish in getting publicity are either a byproduct or the means by which you accomplish your end.

What you are setting out to do is to be very newsworthy. Remember our definition of newsworthiness from Chapter 2:

> *The story that offers the most information with the most*
> *urgency to the most people is the most newsworthy.*

Perhaps we ought to modify this definition slightly to meld with some of what we've learned about how stories are actually selected:

> *The measures of newsworthiness are the interest and*
> *attention of the majority of the audience, which may*
> *arise from any combination of information, urgency,*
> *significance, relevance, and uniqueness.*

Make sense?   Think about whether you agree or disagree with this definition before you accept it.   Is this really newsworthiness being defined, or is it more a definition of spaceworthiness?   Are the two inseparable?   Are the differences significant?   We're going to continue on with the assumption that you agree with this definition, but if you disagree, measure what we offer against your own theories, beliefs, and definitions.   Since so much of what you do in planning and executing these "special events" hinges directly on your understanding of what motivates the media, it's essential that you base your decisions on a definition of newsworthiness in which you are fully and unequivocally confident.

The nature of most "special events" is such that *uniqueness* (or novelty) is the key attribute by which they gain entree into the day's annals.   But it must be a unique event, capable of capturing the interest and attention of a very large group of people in the media audiences.   Often, uniqueness alone is not quite enough to assure the attention of the media, so an activity is sought (such as a charitable involvement) that also offers significance and relevance to the audience.

Specific media have specific requirements.   Television coverage insists on "good pictures," meaning people, action, involvement, and more.   Newspapers are also anxious to find good photos, though action is less important in print.   Radio prefers distinctive sounds, voices of celebrities and VIPs, and so on.   Magazines are like newspapers, in this sense, and hate to be "scooped" on a story, so usually look for a special angle, perhaps a "look behind the scenes" or after-the-fact reactions or results.

But what is it you want your "special event" to accomplish?   Is it enough to expose the name of your company?   Is good will a goal?   Are you solving some specific problem with your image or the way you're perceived by your potential customers or the community?   Are you trying to establish a closer association with some specific product or service?   The first step in deciding what to do for your "special event" is to decide what you want the resulting publicity to accomplish for you.

Then, think about ways that this might be accomplished.   The best way is the one that gets you the most favorable exposure, of course.   Which brings us back to what motivates the media—plus one other consideration, called *profile*.

A *high profile* activity is one that is intended to be obvious and to draw attention; a *low profile* activity is one that's intended to be accomplished quietly, subtly, drawing a minimum of attention (if not shunning attention entirely).   The "special events" we're dealing with here are all high profile activities, of course, since, by our definition, they're intended primarily to draw the attention of the media.   This is not to discourage your company from being involved in low profile activities, especially service activities.   It's just that these don't properly fall within our purview of getting publicity.

So how do you draw the attention of the media?   Here are some hints.

If you can stage your event where there is routinely a large number of people or where (pedestrian) traffic is heavy, you will help fulfill the need of the media to address those stories first which involve the most people.   ("Maybe you saw . . ." is a common television news story introduction.)   The middle of a downtown business district at lunch hour is a prime choice, especially since this also makes you very accessible to camera crews, which are usually dispatched from the downtown or near-downtown offices of the media.   A good second choice is immediately after work, no earlier than 4:00, but with live on-the-scene reports so common these days, you might want to go as late as 6:30.

The more people you can involve, the better.   Some common ploys are:

- Beauty contests
- Downtown block parties
- Barbecue burn-offs
- Dancing in the streets
- Activity-a-thons (walk, bike, crawl, hop, tumble, dance, baton, virtually anything)
- Outdoor exhibits of art or sculpture or contraptions
- Meet-the-celebrity affairs
- Free concerts
- Celebrity races

Flash, flesh, fun, and festivities are the old draws of carnival, and alas, they still work.   But you'll always be a step ahead if you can tie in some nature of charity involvement (proceeds go to the so-and-so fund or foundation), since this adds to the appeal of the story. (Schools call this "borrowed interest," should you decide to study marketing communications or journalism.)   You'll also be able to borrow a little interest if you can involve local celebrities, but don't expect competitors to pick up stories about media celebrities unless theirs are also involved.

Making arrangements is just as much a problem for these special events.   You'll have to begin by contacting the local police depart-ments for their requirements.   Celebrities at local radio and television stations can   usually be reached either directly or through the station promotion department.   National celebrities are a bit more difficult to contact;   begin with the *Celebrity Register* at your local library, the promotion people at their studios or network offices (usually in Los Angeles or Manhattan), or the offices of the Screen Actor's Guild (SAG) for motion picture celebrities, or the American Federation of Television and Radio Artists (AFTRA) for broadcast celebrities in Los Angeles or Manhattan.   (Either will probably ask you to write in care of them, or offer you the name of an agent or manager.)

If you need models, hosts, or hostesses, contact a local modeling agency.   Some will donate services for certain "worthy causes" in which they, too, gain exposure. If there's a contest, you'll need judges. Mix local media celebrities with local political and business celebrities for your best shot at high profile.   If you want to get a charity involved, you'll need to make arrangements with them. They're very cooperative, and can often help with these many arrangements, or, for that matter, you may be doing this for a charity in the first place. Are there special transportation arrangements? Special equipment arrangements you'll need (a public address system, a portable stage, fire control equipment)?   Special services arrangements (security, ambulance, fire, clean-up, technical assistance)?   You'll probably want your own photographer on hand to give you plenty of photos for later releases, or sometimes a magazine or newspaper may ask if you can provide photos when they can't send their own snapshooter out.   You'll be a full-fledged producer of a real event with many people involved (or you may want to hire a producer with some experience in this kind of thing to pull it off for you).   Check with talent and modeling agencies and theater groups for names of such producers.

So be painstaking, cover your flanks, anticipate every need, and allow for every contingency. You might want to consult with your attorney and insurance people about any extra liability you may incur, and buy whatever special coverage you need.

As we've said, media events are never inexpensive, and you want to be certain you can both afford the investment and realize a later return on it.   Good luck.

Interviews

Another way you'll be meeting the press is either in person or as a liaison when they're interested in interviewing you or one of the key people in your company about some specific facet of your activities, attitudes, or accomplishments.   Usually, you can count on excellent exposure as the result of an interview, and should encourage them with full cooperation.

Interviews may happen in person, or may happen over the phone. This is how they're usually initiated.

A call will be from an editor, reporter, author, or writer who has a subject in mind and would like to interview the appropriate person. Assure your full cooperation and find out when you can get back to the caller once the necessary arrangements are made with the interviewee. If a telephone interview is requested, call back with the interviewee on hand (spending your nickel on the call). Once you've reached the interviewer and determined the timing is convenient (or called ahead to make sure the arranged time is convenient), let them take things at their own pace. While you might receive an advance copy of the eventual article, you cannot insist on prior consent or review—freedom of the press is a Constitutional guarantee, you know, and jealously guarded by most professional members of the press. Still, if you've responded openly and cordially, they are likely to cooperate.

If the interview is to be in person, the interviewer may either want to arrange a time to visit (be sure to make a tour of your facilities available and offer your fullest hospitality, within reason) or ask if the interviewee can travel to the interview. Generally, this latter situation is most often the case with broadcast "talk show" formats; there's usually an arrangement made by the broadcast facility for travel and accommodation arrangements. Depending on the ultimate good the coverage can bring you, you may decide to provide your own arrangements, or to send additional people along at your expense.

Public Appearances

There are many times and occasions that will necessitate one or more key persons in your company appearing in public. For some, publicity will be the *raison d'etre* of the event, for others it's just a happy by-product. For example, a company executive may be invited to address a banquet, luncheon or club meeting, a community conference, or a civic organization; these are referred to as *civic involvement*, and the topic of these addresses rarely relates directly to your company and its products or services. Another example involves addressing professional organizations, trade conferences, business groups, industry councils, and so on; these are referred to as *professional involvement* and almost always involve topics relating directly to your company and its products or services. They also rarely stray beyond the prepared material.

A third example involves speeches and demonstrations on your company and its products or services, when presented to the public at large.   These opportunities usually arise during such occasions as an open house, a trade fair or business show, or during special events sponsored by groups of people with an avocational interest in these subjects.   This kind of activity is called either *public awareness* or occasionally *public information*, which, alas, is another term often used to mean public relations or press relations.

A fourth example involves appearances in front of audiences via the broadcast media for purposes of explaining, demonstrating, or promoting the best interests of your company.   This is properly included as a publicity "special event" or, more accurately, a special public relations opportunity.

A fifth example involves statements made to the press by a company executive or spokesperson at the initiative of the press, following an incident or event in which the company was involved.   This is called a *debriefing* and may or may not include an official statement, but will always involve an official response to questions (even if that response is "no comment").

Regardless of which of these examples prompts your need for a spokesperson, it's not a good idea to send anybody in cold.   Prepare ahead of time by planning and filing company statements of policy and position on crucial issues *as these issues appear.* Mark the final position statements as SENSITIVE MATERIAL—COMPANY POLICY OR POSITION STATEMENT—NOT FOR GENERAL RELEASE—NOT FOR PUBLICATION WITHOUT DIRECT EXECUTIVE PERMISSION and keep them in a locked file.

Hold rehearsals, with different individuals playing newspeople or audience at different times; others playing cornered spokesperson, and see how your people respond under fire.   Brief your people on such comments as the following:

> No comment.
>
> I really can't answer that until I've had a chance to study the question more closely.
>
> We are aware of the situation and will be responding shortly with an official statement.
>
> We are not aware of this, and will now be looking into it.

Train and rehearse your spokespeople, and make sure they understand the importance of presenting a dignified, professional image.

(If they don't want to take the time to train and rehearse, enlist the aid of the company principal or attorney to convince them.)   Help them learn to handle unfriendly interviewers or hecklers.   Help them learn how to look collected even when their nerves are frazzled.

A local professor of communications or speech and communications may be able to help you establish a suitable training program for the key people in your company.   If that is you, you may want to consider taking an appropriate night course.

Most interviews are friendly, but like all good Scouts, it pays to "Be Prepared!"

Authorship Programs

Much of what we've discussed so far concerns interfacing with editors and producers.   But now, let's talk about writers and authors, especially those who freelance. These people contribute an astounding amount of editorial material each year to virtually every publication and many broadcasts in the world.   With a little initiative, they could be a tremendous help in your publicity efforts.

Your first contact with a freelancer will probably come when one is preparing an article that requires information about your company. Respond to this first request immediately, fully, and with no strings attached, but ask if you can contact that author later.

Freelance authors are paid by the article upon acceptance (though they often have to wait until well after publication, which may be a year or more later, before they're paid).   In saying *paid by the article* we mean that the check comes from the publication, but the payment is based on the quality and published length of the manuscript and the customary "page rate" of the publication, and there is no other remuneration.   But there can be.

Without unduly unbalancing a magazine's coverage, an author can place an article which shows off your products or services in their best light.   Your competitors may also have to appear in the coverage though.   Remember, freelance authors are not employed by publications and usually their work isn't contracted.   Rather the author will query the editor about an article, the editor will or won't give a go-ahead, and the earliest payment is upon delivery, more often a month or more later.

One aspect of authorship programs is commonly referred to as *ghostwriting.*   A professional author, who may also be a freelancer, prepares material that will be disseminated to a specific publication with the name of one of your company's key people appearing as the author.   This will usually be prompted by a publication's request for a certain type of article from a certain professional at each of several competing companies within an industry—perhaps an article on the state of business from corporate presidents, an article on the state of the art from company engineering directors, an article on how worthwhile a specific trade show is from company marketing directors, and so on.   If any of these people have trouble writing as fluidly and cohesively as a professional author, then ghostwriting is an option worth considering.

Avoiding the Press

As much as it goes against the grain of publicity, there may be times when you need to delay making a statement to the media on a given subject.   About the longest time you can ever hope to buy is a weekend, with 24 hours being a practical maximum.

The best way to avoid the press is to answer the phone and tell the reporter that, off the record, you're working on a specific response, that it will be ready shortly, and that you'll put that reporter at the top of the call-back list, or to call you back at such and such a time.

The second best way is to find an inaccessible corner and ask whoever answers the phone to take messages, and promise that you'll call back first thing in the morning.   And don't take any calls from anybody, because there's no telling who a resourceful reporter might pretend to be.

The worst thing you can do is to continue to avoid the media, since it makes you look guilty of whatever they suspect.   It's much better to admit to discovering the bad deed yourself (or to a key executive or employee having discovered it).   Report that you are moving to take corrective measures, and wish to publicly apologize for your company's unwitting role in the debacle.

The minds of the public, you see, don't long retain memories of small and specific evils, especially where there seems to be a solution couched in the discovery of the problem.   Once it's out in the open, be as active and responsive as possible in solving the problem.   And don't lie, because you can always be caught, and your credibility will suffer long afterward.

It's fruitless to suggest that nothing untoward will ever be discovered, simply because it will always be impossible to please everybody all the time.   But if you are responsible and responsive overall, and if, through publicity, you have established your good reputation and overall long-standing credibility, the wounds will heal quickly.

Isn't it too bad that there really are some desperados out there who make coping with small and often unintentional transgressions so much more difficult for the rest of us.

Tally Ho!

No, we're not riding off to the hounds.   Instead, we're capping off our discussion with some very practical advice.

Carry a pocket calculator, a pocket notebook, two pens, and a major credit card or two (American Express, Carte Blanche, Diners' Club, Visa, or Master Card) everywhere you go.

Meticulously record every detail of every expenditure you make, including the date, the business purpose, any portion that was not for business, the amount, any other people involved (number and names plus company affiliations), tips, everything.   And save every receipt. (I nearly forgot, since it's in my blood by now. Make it second nature to always insist on a receipt.)

Here's why.

If you're in business for yourself, the IRS will require this kind of information before they'll allow you to deduct lunches, extravaganzas, or even phone calls. Consult your tax accountant for specifics.

If you work for someone else, your boss needs the same information for the same reason. Many companies have travel and entertainment expense reporting forms. Procure a small supply of blanks for yourself, and always have one or two along when you're on the road to use as a worksheet for the report you'll finish when you get back to the office.

If any portion of your out-of-pocket expenditures can be considered a charitable contribution—consult your tax accountant for specific advice—good records can help make you eligible for a deduction on your personal taxes next April.

So keep an accurate tally. It can lead to a brilliant deduction.

5

The Release

Who. What. When. Where. Why. How. The six proverbial elements of news are the six crucial ingredients in a news release. But don't forget the spice. In this chapter, you'll learn everything you need to know about how to write and prepare a release, except which words to choose. Even if that is a modest exaggeration, it will help get you used to the confident attitude you need to convey in a release.

Putting Together a Release Package

When you're involved with an ongoing publicity program, there are many types of releases which you will issue routinely. Announcements of products, personnel, pricing, and events, as we've discussed, are some possibilities. But there are a few announcements which occur each year that are particularly significant to both your company and the media. When these major events occur, you will be issuing more than one "routine" release, of course.

We're going to take this opportunity to introduce the concept of a release package—or "press kit"—to illustrate the way the how of a story is handled. You'll recognize that the how element can be integrated into every release, as it should be, but this approach can help you understand it a little better.

The elements of a release package usually include:

1. The "cover" release.
2. The "backgrounder" release.

3. The "remarks" (or "quotes") release.

4. The text of any statement or speech at the event.

5. "Bio" releases—biographies of significant people or companies.

6. Supporting documentation or literature.

7. Pertinent photos.

The "cover" release is the basic release that gives the fundamental facts of your story—the who, what, where, when, why, and how. It should be capable of standing alone, if need be; that is, able to tell your whole story with no need for additional information. If you could only send out one release, this would be it. But we'll see why these other elements in the release package are also good to include.

The "backgrounder" release, or releases, (you may want to include separate backgrounders on each part of your announcement if the subject is complex) provides the editor or reporter with additional information to put the story in perspective. There might be a backgrounder giving the history of the organization or key, salient points about it. There might be a backgrounder explaining a given product category. If you are introducing an electrically powered motorcycle, for example, you might include a backgrounder that charts the history and progress of electric vehicles of all kinds. There might be backgrounders explaining the problem that your announcement is intended to solve. In the case of our electric motorcycle, there might be a backgrounder on rising fuel costs, the comparative costs of operating gasoline versus electric motorcycles, or on the impact of the vehicle on annual national energy usage.

Other backgrounders might tell the story of the research and development efforts behind the announcement, or the successes and failures of earlier attempts to produce such a product or service. A backgrounder might provide a simplified explanation of the technology that lets your gizmo perform its unique tricks. ("How our lunchbox-size laboratory helps robot spacecraft search for life on other worlds" or "How your body can provide the energy to run a wristwatch without batteries.")

The "remarks" or "quotes" release or releases give your company officials and influential, outside support people a forum for commenting on the significance of your news. If your company is introducing a new highway safety device, add comments on its innovation from your company president and on its universal appeal from your company marketing vice president. You might even want to include the comments of a police chief who has had a chance to preview the device in operation, the comments of a key legislator who supports the development of this kind of product, and so on.

In addition to these—which can have been made at any time previous to your official announcement—you will want to include the full text of a statement or speech made to the press. This the only way to assure that any quotes that appear in the media coverage of your event will be accurate.

If the people and personalities involved are significant to the event, you may also want to include a brief "bio" (biography) of each. While you probably know these people well, the media might not, and the better they understand the who behind the what, the better your chances of fair coverage. Similarly, as we said when discussing backgrounders, a brief story of each of the companies involved (it might be a merger announcement, for example) helps the media report your story fully and fairly.

You may want to include previously-printed literature that provides additional information in any of these areas. This might include product literature, annual reports, "how-to" pamphlets or brochures, reprints of relevant articles (be sure you secure permission, or buy copies of the whole publication and bookmark the specific article), operating manuals, and so on.

All pertinent photos are invaluable in a release package. They are given their own chapter, following this one.

Now we will look more specifically at some of the many details of a release.

Stationery

How do you say, "This is important. This is significant. This is news." without sending a messenger with each release you issue? One way is to let your letterhead do it, but this is just one of the jobs your letterhead needs to do.

Who are you? Where are you? How can an editor get in touch with you? How professional are you? Your company? Your publicity program? These are all things your letterhead can help convey.

Does your company already have a letterhead? If so, you should be able to skip many preliminary steps and simply adapt your current letterhead to the special needs of a release letterhead; if not, don't skip this section.

News from

FOR FURTHER INFORMATION:

Richard G. Williford
Dept. 703 - Public Relations
SEARS, ROEBUCK AND CO.
Sears Tower
Chicago, Illinois 60684
(312) 875-8313

Sears new "RoadHandler TR" is a milestone in Sears tire development history that has made the company sales and quality a substantial factor in a passenger car tire market that currently sells some 190,000,000 units to generate sales in excess of $6 billion.

Sears, Roebuck and Co. got rolling in the replacement tire business with the introduction of the automobile tire in the 1914 spring general catalog. Four styles offered then ranged in price from $8.27 to $47.78 for the casings and from $2.00 to $8.00 for the inner tubes.

Sears gained momentum by offering truck tires in 1924, snow tires in 1933, tubeless tires in 1955, and its famous steel-belted radial tires in 1966.

While the company wasn't first to offer a radial-ply tire, Sears popularized this revolutionary new construction among American motorists. The radial's legendary mileage -- although warranted for 40,000 miles -- not infrequently exceeds 100,000 miles before replacement is necessary.

Today, radials are standard equipment on many new cars. Radial tires represent almost 40 per cent of Sears and the industry's tire sales with projected market share to more than 60 per cent in 1983.

Sears new RoadHandler TR highlights a complete line of truck and passenger car tires with bias ply, bias belted and radial ply, with steel or aramid fiber belting, designed to meet the tire needs of nearly any car, truck or van.

# # #

F51144

Figure 5-1.   Three separate letterheads used by Sears, including a general format, a men's wear format, and a children's wear format. (Courtesy Sears, Roebuck & Co.)

If "investment" is the key word in your fashion wardrobe, consider outerwear as a "blue chip" selection. Styling and construction techniques, along with layering, have greatly increased its length of service and its adaptability.

"The line-up of Fall '80 outerwear offers a lot of flexibility," says Paul Rogers, fashion director for Sears Men's Store. "The kind of flexibility that can really work with a man's lifestyle and wardrobe."

A lightweight survival jacket or slicker is almost seasonless, depending on the types of clothing worn underneath.

Leather jackets with blazer styling can function as lightweight outerwear and then move easily inside and work as a sporty blazer with slacks.

A bomber jacket or split-cowhide jacket can be worn through late fall and again in early spring.

And the classic business look -- a pile-lined trenchcoat -- works from November to March.

"Outerwear is no longer just a buffer from the elements," concluded Rogers. "It makes a very visible fashion statement that ties the wardrobe pieces together."

# # #

Figure 5-1 *(Continued)*

Sears **the Children's Store**

While blue jeans were once the "uniform" for children, they're now getting some stiff competition from other items of apparel. Chino and corduroy pants, dresses, skirts, sweaters and blouses are very much in evidence this back-to-school season.

This shift toward more traditional dressing should please Mom for a number of reasons. According to Jack Simpson, fashion director for Sears children's wear, "The preppy look offers classic styling with lasting appeal. Not only does it provide a neat appearance, but because of its timeless look and quality features, it represents a good value for the consumer."

On the heels of the preppy look is activewear in three distinct fabrications -- sweatshirt fleecing, velour and terry, points out Simpson. On the jeans scene, the interest is on the back pocket with colorful character appliques. For smallfries, the interest is up front with colorful character apparel featuring the likes of Miss Piggy, Road Runner and Snoopy.

Navy, red, burgundy, rust and tan color the traditional classics and bright color slicing puts it mark on tops and outerwear for toddlers through teens. Fake fur hooded coats and sporty jackets round out the outerwear picture for fall.

# # #

Figure 5-1 *(Continued)*

The fundamental parts of any letterhead are the company name, logo, address, and phone numbers, plus teletypewriter access (TWX or Telex) numbers, if applicable.   These are also musts for the letterhead you develop for your release.   The term *logo*, by the way, is short for logotype and refers to the distinctive design associated with, designed around, or incorporating the company's name—for example, McDonald's "golden arches" design, Westinghouse's distinctive circled "W," Lincoln-Mercury's "cat,"   Kodak's red and yellow square, CBS's "eye," Coca-Cola's distinctive script lettering style for the words "Coca-Cola," and so forth.

Creating your own logo can be as simple as consulting a local typesetter in search of a unique typeface that can be used (or slightly modified—like all professionals, they have a few tricks up their rolled-up sleeves).   Or you can hire the services of a professional graphics designer, whose business it is, in part, to create logos.

If you consult a graphics designer, or even a typesetter, be prepared to spring for a lunch and maybe a bottle of firewater later, in addition to the charges you incur.   Be sure to discuss the layout of your letterhead when you do.   Overall, it's unimportant where on the page (except the middle, of course) you want to put the various pieces of information, but it is important that all the information be there and presented in a dignified, professional, and attractive manner.

The decisions about what goes where, what sizes of type you want to use, what type styles, and so on, all make up the layout of the page. Another important consideration is which and how many colors to use.   If you use only black, it will be easier to reproduce your prepared releases later;   although there are relatively inexpensive ways to reproduce any release on any letterhead.   Also, the more colors in your letterhead, the more expensive it will be to have printed.

You have a few options in preparing your letterhead.   One is on whether information that your release requires be made part of the letterhead or printed when the *copy*, or the words you write for each release, is printed.

Another option is the way you announce that this is a news release. You could simply say "NEWS!" on the letterhead, and add either "FOR IMMEDIATE RELEASE" or "FOR RELEASE ON OR AFTER (date)" when you print the release copy.   This gives editors advance notification of an announcement, and still controls the actual date of the publication of your news.

Another is the name and phone number, including any extension, if appropriate, or a direct phone line number of the person editors should contact for additional information. This should be appropriately labeled within the *body* of the release. This is another term for the copy; a third variation is *body copy*. You will need to spell out whom readers should contact (where and how, including address, phone, and hours available) for additional information. For example, you might include something like this either above the headline or following the main body copy:

FOR ADDITIONAL INFORMATION:

EDITORS' CONTACT, First name   Last name, (Area code) Phone number

READERS' CONTACT, First name   Last name, (Area code) Phone number

If one person has primary responsibility for providing additional information for editors, that person's name and phone number (face it, it's probably you) can be incorporated into the letterhead itself. Whether or not the same person is always responsible for providing additional information to readers, that person's name, address, and number should be incorporated into the body copy.

By the way, there are many times when the person providing additional information to editors will not be at the same address as the company. This is the case, for example, when an advertising or publicity agency prepares releases for its clients. In this instance, the company's name should always be made a prominent and integral part of the letterhead. The full name and address of the agency as well as the name and phone number of the person for editors to contact should be included, but subordinately (any other arrangement would be, professionally speaking, insubordinate).

The many examples of professionally prepared news releases included throughout this book are reproduced exactly as they were disseminated (except for colors on the original letterhead, which are reproduced here as black). This is to show you the elements these organizations incorporate into their letterhead designs.

The original press releases are always 8½" x11" and you are strongly urged not to vary from this standard. We will discuss the paper that releases are printed on in Chapter 7.

While we have been speaking primarily of one piece of letterhead stationery, there are actually three that should concern us. Since the letterhead information requires so much room, you should consider a more modest layout for the second and following pages of your releases. You might simply include something like NEWS FROM

Figure 5-2.   Letterhead design is translated into distinctive envelopes. (Courtesy Sears, Roebuck & Co.)

RESEARCH
EDUCATION
PUBLIC AFFAIRS

FOOD MARKETING INSTITUTE

1750 K STREET, N.W., WASHINGTON, D.C. 20006   TEL (202) 452-8444   TELEX: 892722 FMI USA WSH

FOR IMMEDIATE RELEASE

Contact: Jack Cergol   Jeffrey R. Prince
          Manager,   Vice President,
          Communications   Communications

<u>FMI Bottle Handling Study Cites Increased Costs for Supermarkets</u>

Washington, D.C. October 29...Food retailers may be spending as
much as 2.372 cents for redeeming each soft drink and beer container
taken into their store, according to a recent study done by the
Food Marketing Institute (FMI).

The report was released at the Institute's Public Affairs Conference
held in San Francisco earlier this month, and according to FMI
Senior Vice President Timothy M. Hammonds, bottle handling costs
add to the overall costs of doing business in the supermarket
industry.

Hammonds said that the purpose in ordering the study was two-fold:
"We wanted to develop a figure that can be used when it is
necessary to fight the passage of deposit legislation, and we
wanted to discover the cost of efficiently handling returnables
when we are required to do so by law."

He added that during the 1970's state and federal regulations
regarding bottle handling significantly affected the industry's
operating results. "This report makes it clear that the bottle bills,

More

Figure 5-3.   FMI uses the simplest following page letterhead—plain paper.   This
release was printed on both sides of a single sheet. (Courtesy Food Marketing
Institute)

96

Bottle handling
Page Two

currently being considered by so many state legislatures, would
increase costs for supermarkets and for their customers in a
significant way," he said.

The report estimates that at 2.373 cents per container a 24-bottle
case of soft drinks would cost 56.95 cents to redeem; however,
these figures could vary with individual companies.

The primary value of the returnable beverage container study is
providing retailers with worksheets they can use to determine
how much their firms are spending to redeem bottles and cans.

Additionally, the report measures only the tangible costs directly
related to handling bottles -- labor, allocated floor space,
additional sanitation facilities, carrying costs of deposit
inventory, breakage and pilferage. The largest cost factor is
employee time required to handle returned containers. Intangible
factors, such as store disruption, were not quantified in the
study.

The stores studied in the report are located in states now requiring
mandatory deposits: Connecticut, Michigan, Oregon, Iowa, Virginia
and Maine.

The FMI Bottle Handling Study and worksheets will be available
in November from FMI, at $7.50 for members and $15 for non-members.

Figure 5-3 *(Continued)*

(company name) in one line at the top or bottom of the page.   In addition, you might want to consider using a distinctive news release design on the mailing envelopes for your releases and photos.   This could be as simple as a rubber stamp (the bigger the better) that says NEWS, or as ornate as a modification of your layout, in whole or in part.

Since you will usually be enclosing a photo with your release, you will want to use an envelope that's at least 8½" x 11", and you may find it easier to go to 9" x 12".   Be sure to include cardboard for safeguarding any photographs.

Postal requirements dictate that your return address be in the upper left-hand corner, reading from left to right.   Postage should be in the upper right-hand corner, and the name and address of the recipient clearly identifiable lower on the page, reading from left to right. Outside of this, you can call any edge you choose the top edge.

You may want to preprint the legend FIRST CLASS MAIL, which is helpful, and possibly URGENT or DATED MATERIALS, which is seldom helpful.

If your publicity program involves a large number of releases to a large list of people, you may want to consider using a heat-sealed polybag envelope, at only a fraction of the cost of standard paper envelopes.   Multiply the number of releases by the number of people over any given length of time to get an idea of the number of pieces of front page and envelope stationery you'll need.   To make the best use of these heat-sealed envelopes, you should provide return address and mailing label information on an inserted sheet.   If this sheet doubles as the stiffener for your photo (using a white cardboard stock), you'll cut down on both the expense of stuffing, and on the time it takes to stuff each envelope.   If you use metered mail, your imprint can be made on the sheet inside the polybag envelope; if you use stamps, these must be applied to the outside.   Consult your local postal authorities and the people who sell these see-through envelopes for details.

If your mailing list is limited and you often include a photo and a two-or-more-page release,   you may want to consider using United Parcel Service (UPS) instead of the mails.   The only way to   tell whether or not you'll save money is to compare first class   United States Postal Service (USPS) rates for the weight of your packaged release and the delivery-distance zone (which is used if it's over a pound for the USPS) with UPS rates, based on how many names on your mailing list are in each distance category.   In short, find out what it will cost to send them by UPS and compare that   to what it will cost to mail them.   Keep in mind that the two primary considerations for charges, which may or may not vary from piece to piece, are weight and distance.   While you're checking, look into the difference, if any, in the speed of delivery (UPS vs. USPS).

Okay, we've gone over most of what you need to know in order to develop news release letterhead stationery, but we've left out one consideration.

If you're working on a limited budget—for your club, for example—and feel a little put out over all this talk about graphic designers, layouts, typesetters, and printed stationery, relax.   You're in a different category.   In fact, many editors would be wary if they saw a small, local organization communicating on expensive stationery.

All you need to get the job done is a typewriter capable of making clearly-formed characters.   You'll be surprised at the improvements a new ribbon and a little cleaning can make on the old workhorse you have around somewhere.   You will still want to include the letterhead information we discussed, but just type it at the top of the page.

Spacing is also very important to the look of your releases.   You'll want to leave about an inch margin all around.   Your letterhead information could be single spaced, but your body copy should be double spaced.   Skip four to six spaces between your letterhead and the beginning of body copy or headline, if you include one (it's recommended).

Also, if you have a business of your own that you're just getting off the ground, most editors will understand if you, too, go the all-typewriter route.   Just don't be pretentious; your stationery will give the lie to your bravado.   Remember, a small organization can impress an editor as being sincere, professional, and "real" by simply keeping these first "typewriter-letterhead" releases very matter-of-fact in content, and continuing the same kind of body copy in your first letterhead.   It's the American dream—a company that starts small and by hard work and determination writes its own success story. It's more important, however, to create an honest impression than a successful one.

Before the Headline

You don't want to clutter up your release with so much extraneous information that the headline doesn't appear until the bottom of page 1.   There are, however, a few things an editor may find useful, both now and when searching through filed releases later.

One of these is the date of the release.   It's best to date a release the day it's mailed, not the day it's written or printed. The date should be the top line of printed copy following the preprinted letterhead information.

RESEARCH
EDUCATION
PUBLIC AFFAIRS

FOOD MARKETING INSTITUTE

1750 K STREET, N.W., WASHINGTON, D.C. 20006   TEL. (202) 452-8444   TELEX: 892722 FMI USA WSH

FOR IMMEDIATE RELEASE

Contact: Jack Cergol   Jeffrey Prince
           Manager, Communications   Vice President, Communications

CPI Finally Reflects Food Price Increases

     Washington D.C. September 23..."It has taken over two months, but the Consumer Price Index (CPI) is finally reflecting the food price increases predicted earlier this year by the U.S. Department of Agriculture (USDA)," according to Robert O. Aders, president of Food Marketing Institute.

     Aders said the the government's producer price index, the yardstick for measuring the cost of producing food, rose 8.2 percent for consumer foods during July and August, but that, "there has always been a lag between increases and decreases in producer prices and similar price movements at the consumer level; we are beginning to see those increases now."

     The 2.3 percent increase for food as reflected by the CPI comes as no real suprise since USDA has been warning the American public that increases in food prices would come as a result of the heat wave and wide spread drought that began in mid-June, coupled with a reduction of domestic food supplies.

     "Pork and poultry producers have cut back on their production of broilers, turkeys and eggs because of the low prices they are getting for those items, and foreign demand for American crops is up because of poor harvests around the world.

                     (More)

Figure 5-4.   A highly newsworthy release. The letterhead helps. Can you see how? (Courtesy Food Marketing Institute)

100

"The drought devastated crops and livestock in the Farm Belt of the nation. Preliminary USDA reports indicate for example, that fruits and vegetable canning crops will be 15% under 1979 crop figures, providing no extra carry-over into the 1980-81 year," Aders said.

The FMI president cited other USDA projections that indicate a tough year for food prices: corn at 6.5 billion bushels -- 16 percent less than the 1979 crops.

"If this year's corn crop materializes, it would be very ample for our own needs, however, foreign demand will cut heavily into this supply," he noted.

The USDA expects a 22 million ton reduction in available corn feed grain stocks -- the largest year-to-year decline on record.

This year's soybean crop is projected to be 17 percent smaller than last year's; and red meat and poultry, according to USDA, will be down in the third and fourth quarters.

The government agency sees the fourth quarter broiler production decreasing by 7 to 9 percent and pork reduction down by 2 to 4 percent. More recent projections, however, indicate a greater reduction in the pork supply in 1981.

"The cattle industry went through a period of liquidation starting in 1976, and we are still at the low end of the cycle with beef still relatively scarce and expensive," Aders said.

(more)

Figure 5-4 *(Continued)*

101

```
CPI
Page Three


     In addition, he indicated that the food supply problem was

only part of food inflation and that handling costs -- the cost

of transporting, processing, storing and retailing food -- have

increased at a rate comparable to general inflation.

     "Handling costs in the food industry are directly linked

to the general inflation rate.  Despite massive cost containment

programs like scanning, energy conservation or central meat cut-

ting, the rate of increase in handling costs may not slow down

until the government finds a way to curtail inflation", he said.


                         ####
```

Figure 5-4 *(Continued)*

Next comes the release information.   If FOR IMMEDIATE RE-LEASE has been preprinted as part of your stationery, you don't need to repeat it here, but you can if you like.   This line might read FOR IMMEDIATE RELEASE or NOT FOR RELEASE BEFORE (date) or HOLD FOR RELEASE (date).   You can see here where the term release came from; it is a "letting go" or transfer of news from a source to a publication or broadcaster.   Protocol within the industry is rigidly adhered to, and a request to delay the release of information to the public is generally respected.

Some publicity operations include the names and phone numbers of editorial and reader contact people at the top of a release; some at the bottom.   There are a few advantages to including these at the top.   One is that no secretary will then leave them out in going to one more page; another is that it makes them easier for an editor to find.   But the choice is yours.

Another option is the statement PHOTO(S) ENCLOSED.   An editor knows a photo on sight and won't mistake the one you've enclosed for backing board, so this statement is generally redundant.   On the other hand, if the editor sees the statement and you have not enclosed a photo in that particular envelope, the editor will know to call and ask for the missing picture.   Again, this PHOTO ENCLOSED statement can be placed either above the headline or after the body copy.

One more option you have is whether or not to include a release number.   Editors may use a release number that you provide as a reference, should there be any questions.   ("I'm calling about your release number 251 on the new miniature gizmo.")   More important, it will be a tremendous aid to you in keeping track of your publicity releases as they're being prepared, and again later as you learn to use them to gauge your results. (See Chapter 9 for details.)   You may find it helpful to use the last two digits of the year in your release number, with two or three additional digits providing sequence information. The 150th release issued during 1991 would be numbered 91150, for example.   Use this or any other scheme that helps, but do work with a method in mind—and on paper.

The Headline

The most effective words in headlines are "announces," "new," and comparative adjectives like   "better" or "more" (often preferred to superlatives like "best" or "most" for reasons of credibility).   For example:

COMPANY ANNOUNCES NEW ROUNDER WHEEL

The headline, as we've discussed,   may be the only part of your release some editors read.   While releases are seldom accepted on the basis of a headline, they are often rejected because of a headline. Let's say your company is called XYZ Corporation, that one of your major activities is manufacturing light bulbs, and your engineering design lab has just developed an exciting new bulb that uses less than 10% of the power of other light bulbs, delivers more light for the power it uses, lasts 10 to 15 years in normal service, and will cost only 20¢ per bulb at retail.   Here are some alternate headlines for this same story.

XYZ ANNOUNCES NEW LIGHT BULB

NEW LIGHT BULB FROM XYZ BOASTS HIGHER   EF-FICIENCY

XYZ REVOLUTIONIZES LIGHT BULB

XYZ ANNOUNCES BREAKTHROUGH IN LIGHT BULB TECHNOLOGY

"NEW 20¢ LIGHT BULB LASTS 15 YEARS, USES LESS ENERGY, " SAYS XYZ

NEW XYZ LIGHT BULB MAY BE "BAD FOR COMPETITORS"

TODAY'S LIGHTBULB OBSOLETE WHEN NEW XYZ DESIGN APPEARS

NEW XYZ BREAKTHROUGH ANNOUNCED: LIGHT BULBS TO COST LESS, LAST LONGER, USE LESS ENERGY

XYZ ANNOUNCES "BIGGEST BREAKTHROUGH IN LIGHT BULBS SINCE EDISON"

XYZ REINVENTS LIGHT BULB: "DESIGN BREAKTHROUGH TO BRING 20¢ LIGHT BULBS WITH 15-YEAR LIFE, HIGHER ENERGY EFFICIENCY," COMPANY PRESIDENT ANNOUNCES

Let's take our example, look at the headlines and see what's right and wrong about each of them.

XYZ ANNOUNCES NEW LIGHT BULB.   That's true, this is an announcement of a new light bulb, but isn't there more to it than that?   This isn't a change in the shape of the glass, the frosting on the bulb, or anything quite as routine as this headline would imply.   And after all, if the headline makes your announcement seem routine, who could blame an editor for assuming that your announcement is fairly routine.   Some examples we've given would make every network news program, newspaper, trade publication, business publication, and more all over the world; it would cause a panic among investors in XYZ's competitors, a ballooning of XYZ stocks, and probably Federal intervention.

Look at it this way: Would you read a story on page 38 of your morning paper if it were only a few inches long, with XYZ ANNOUNCES NEW LIGHT BULB as its headline?   This certainly sounds like a ho-hum story, and that's exactly the way an editor is likely to perceive it.

Remember, nobody owes you a reading. You have to earn it. You have to lure your reader into wanting to read more; to know more. And then you have to deliver the goods.

NEW LIGHT BULB FROM XYZ BOASTS HIGHER EFFICIENCY. Well, we're getting closer.   But of all the product claims, is higher efficiency the most newsworthy choice?   Wouldn't it be stronger to say NEW LIGHT BULB FROM XYZ LASTS 15 YEARS? Or, perhaps, NEW LIGHT BULB FROM XYZ COSTS LESS THAN 20¢? Remember, it's always a good idea to lead with a benefit that your announcement signifies, but it's important to recognize and lead with your strongest benefit first.   If there's a toss-up, put them both in. In this case, the headline might become NEW HIGHER EFFICIENCY LIGHT BULB FROM XYZ USES LESS POWER, DELIVERS MORE LIGHT, LASTS FIFTEEN YEARS, COSTS 20¢. Or even better, NEW LIGHT BULB LASTS 15 YEARS, SAVES ENERGY, SELLS FOR 20¢. When you're dealing with a resale price (you may think of it as a retail price, but always say resale, for reasons we'll discuss in a moment), the phrase "sells for" is a lot more accurate than the word "costs."   This is always true unless you are actually referring to the manufacturer's or dealer's cost, which is marked up before final sale.   Also, in this case, while all three of the mentioned characteristics are significant, "lasts 15 years" is the most unique.   And uniqueness is one of the tests of newsworthiness.

XYZ REVOLUTIONIZES LIGHT BULB.   This could well be a valid headline, but lacks substance.   In order to add to its substance and credibility, we can use a second-level headline, called a *subhead*. The subhead allows us to expand on the idea presented in the headline without forcing the reader to read the body copy for the high points of the message.   For example, the head and subhead of this release might look something like this:

XYZ REVOLUTIONIZES LIGHT BULB
Breakthrough design boasts 15-year life, delivers ten times more light per Watt, yet will sell for just 20¢

And if there's more than one group of key points you want to make, you can use more than one subhead.   For example, we can expand the headline this way:

XYZ REVOLUTIONIZES LIGHT BULB
Breakthrough design boasts 15-year life, delivers ten times more light per Watt, yet will sell for just 20¢.

Company offers to license competitors to use new process, several have already signed.

Production to begin in July, stores will have bulbs by September.

If this is the case, there should be corresponding sections of body copy attached. An editor would expect a release with this headline to be between 4 and 10 (too long for most releases) pages.

An alternative way of handling this much information is to include the headline and subheads on a cover sheet attached to three separate releases, each with the same main head and one of the three subheads. Each may also be accompanied by a different photo. At this point, you have developed what is referred to as a *release package* or *press kit*. Generally, if a story is big enough to warrant a press kit, and has enough ramifications, there will probably be cause to hold a press conference or similar media event. (See Chapter 4.) The point here is to use multiple subheads only for big stories; those important and pressing enough to merit special treatment and substantial press kits. If there are that many good things to communicate about a less pressing announcement you have to make, start with a general release giving the broad picture, and follow up with additional releases, mailed separately, featuring the secondary aspects of the story. This is an effective way to get more exposure for your story.

XYZ ANNOUNCES BREAKTHROUGH IN LIGHT BULB TECHNOLOGY. Our fourth headline has a fault of its own, one you may be able to guess by now. Think about it. Take a moment to consider what the headline is and isn't saying before you go to the next paragraph.

Got it? The breakthrough in light bulb technology is a *feature*, not a *benefit*. This breakthrough, in and of itself, is meaningless to the person who uses these new light bulbs. But let's see how much more effective the headline becomes when we plug in the benefits we've already identified:

XYZ BREAKTHROUGH IN LIGHT BULB TECHNOLOGY BRINGS NEW BULBS THAT LAST 15 YEARS, GIVE TEN TIMES THE LIGHT PER WATT, SELL FOR JUST 20¢

We also broke one of our first rules: Dropping the word "announces." So much for rules; they're just rules of thumb here, and you will need to bring all the good judgment and imagination you can to your publicity program if it is going to really perform for you.

"NEW 20¢ LIGHT BULB LASTS 15 YEARS, USES LESS ENERGY," SAYS XYZ.   We're getting closer to a good, newsworthy, benefit-driven headline, but this is written the way it might appear in print, not the way it should appear as a headline for your release. Drop the last thought and you have a very clean, very strong headline: NEW 20¢ LIGHT BULB LASTS 15 YEARS, USES LESS ENERGY.

NEW XYZ LIGHT BULB MAY BE "BAD FOR COMPETITORS." Is this the most important thing there is about your new light bulb? Probably not, though it may be an important positioning statement to the trade (your dealers, distributors, and the people who sell your products to their end users).   If you are careful to limit distribution of this kind of "nyaah-nyaah" release to the trade, you can use this kind of headline, with one modification: put the statement in the mouth of a company sales manager or executive.   NEW XYZ LIGHT BULB MAY BE "BAD FOR COMPETITORS," SAYS SALES V.P. is a more professional way of getting the same strong positioning accomplished.

TODAY'S LIGHT BULB OBSOLETE WHEN NEW XYZ DESIGN APPEARS.   Bunk.   This doesn't ring true, and there's no expressed or implied benefit in this obvious overstatement.   There is a way to turn these negatives around, however.   "COST, ENERGY, AND MAINTENANCE SAVINGS WITH NEW XYZ DESIGN MAY SOMEDAY MAKE TODAY'S LIGHT BULB OBSOLETE," PREDICTS COMPANY PRESIDENT (or other quotable source).   Even with the turnaround we've accomplished by rewriting the headline, the "possible future" implications of the headline strongly suggest an opinion, and opinions must be attributed to a source.   The best way to accomplish this is to include a lengthy quote (at least several paragraphs) from some knowledgeable, credible source.   So much the better if it's an expert from outside your own company and you can easily establish his or her credentials for the reader.

NEW XYZ BREAKTHROUGH ANNOUNCED: LIGHT BULBS TO COST LESS, LAST LONGER, USE LESS ENERGY.   What more could we ask for?   Here's a headline that includes "new," "announced," the company name, and three strong benefits!

Well, we might ask for a shorter headline.   While it isn't mandatory to keep headlines short, a short headline is more likely to sink into an editor's mind and stay there, which gives your release a slightly better chance of running.   Also, since editors will use, edit, or adapt your headline, for their coverage of your story, you'll be helping to make that coverage easier and have a closer hand in how the eventual story will be headlined.   One option is: "NEW LIGHT BULBS TO COST LESS, LAST LONGER, USE LESS ENERGY," ANNOUNCES XYZ.   Or even better: NEW XYZ LIGHT BULBS COST LESS, LAST LONGER, USE LESS ENERGY.   It's worth taking the time to rewrite your headlines, for all the reasons given above.

XYZ ANNOUNCES "BIGGEST BREAKTHROUGH IN LIGHT BULBS SINCE EDISON."   This headline is a good way to announce the breakthrough with a significant quote (as might be made during a special conference or convention).   But why would you open with a quote instead of a product-oriented announcement?   One reason is that you want to attract attention now for a future announcement of major proportions.   Releases that do this are called *teasers*, and they rarely say more than "something's coming."   Running a teaser is like crying "wolf"—you'd better be prepared to back it up or you'll lose credibility.

Teaser release copy would probably say something like there's been a major breakthrough in the laboratory, and while you are not yet free to release any details, there will be a major announcement in the near future.   This statement may be couched in any other bit of news, or even more routine reporting.   Teaser releases do not necessarily have to be picked up and run in order to get their job done; they pave the way for the news to come, alert editors that something is cooking, and help you get more and better coverage when the big day finally arrives.

"XYZ REINVENTS LIGHT BULB: DESIGN BREAKTHROUGH TO BRING 20¢ LIGHT BULB WITH 15-YEAR LIFE, HIGHER ENERGY EFFICIENCY," COMPANY PRESIDENT ANNOUNCES. This is a good, solid headline, if a bit long.   It could run in virtually any publication, but the astute editor will read between the lines and know that the primary reason for this release is to boost the company's image with investors.

Whoa!   Where did that one come from?   Maybe you thought this is precisely the kind of headline you would write, but you had no intention of leaving that kind of impression!

Let's get out the scalpels and dissect this animal to see how the news bone is connected to the stock market bone.   The key news in the release is contained in the central wording, DESIGN BREAK-THROUGH TO BRING 20¢ LIGHT BULB WITH 15-YEAR LIFE, HIGHER ENERGY EFFICIENCY.   This alone would have been an excellent headline, and editors know that.   Now look at the wording that's wrapped around this nugget (the news bone, if you will).

XYZ REINVENTS LIGHT BULB is a statement of corporate ac-
complishment.   In and of itself it's a promise of a new invention; a
new design of a mainstream product.   And that alone is enough to
prompt at least some investor interest.   It also contains enough overstatement (or *puffery,* as it's called) that it carries a feeling of some-
body-trying-to-sell-something-to-somebody.

And the clincher is " . . .COMPANY PRESIDENT ANNOUNCES."
Announces?   To whom?   Why the company president?   Was it a
formal announcement?   About the only group to whom a company
president would announce a major breakthrough is stockholders
at an annual meeting.   If the group consisted of dealers, the announcement would probably have been made by a sales manager; if it was
a technical forum or conference, the announcement probably would
have been made by an engineer, a designer, or research and development director.

Still, many novices make the mistake of embellishing their headlines.   And misinterpretation of intentions by an editor isn't the
only pitfall.   If the XYZ company were publicly traded as a stock on
any exchange, the Securities and Exchange Commission might take
a more than usual interest in what could be interpreted as an attempt
to "kite the stock" (inflate its price by promoting trading of the stock
in anticipation of a major change in the company's market position).
Other pitfalls may befall other unintentional implications, so you are
advised to keep the statements in your headlines simple and direct.

These ten headline approaches to a single announcement illustrate
most of the principles you will want to follow or avoid.   In writing a
headline, follow this procedure:

1. Determine the most significant benefit your most important reader will derive from the effects of the news behind your announcement.

2. Try to state it in five words or less.

3. Ask yourself if your statement is meaningful to someone not
   closely involved with your product or your company.   If
   not, go to step 4; if so, you're done.

4. Allow yourself one more word.   Then repeat step 3.

Contact: Jack Cergol   Jeffrey R. Prince
          Manager,   Vice President,
          Communication   Communications

<u>FMI's Aders Urges 'Productivity Improvement Systems' to IBM Sales Group</u>

Washington, D.C. June 25...In an address before the Advanced Grocery
Workshop of the IBM Corporation recently, Food Marketing Institute
President Robert O. Aders suggested that the sales force
develop productivity improvement systems for their equipment as
opposed to simply "selling scanning equipment to grocers."

"I think you could sell more scanners by selling productivity
than you can just demonstrating machinery," Aders said.

To emphasize his point, Aders used the example of the "data
transmission system" or computer hook-up from the distributor's
computer directly to the supplier's, to place orders. "This
system would promote a tremendous increase in efficiency and
decrease paperwork, while saving approximately $300 million per
year," he added.

FMI and GMA got involved in the data transmission system project
nearly four years ago. A feasibility study into the system has been
completed and a pilot project will be constructed within a year.
"However," Aders said, "no equipment manufacturer has been involved
with the system as yet."

More

Figure 5-5.   A good example of a strong first paragraph that helps add newsworthiness to a "quotes" release. (Courtesy Food Marketing Institute)

Stressing productivity improvement, the FMI president urged
the sales people to "stop selling equipment and start helping
food retailers develop systems which make your equipment absolutely
essential for every operator."

In addition, he said IBM could help retailers while promoting
their sales by "selling" the concept of checkout scanners to the
consumer.

"I know you think about your product in terms of your customers,
but have you been thinking in terms of our customers?" he asked
rhetorically.

Aders had praise for IBM's award-winning television ad for
scanning saying that new technology has a tendency to frighten
the public unless its operation is carefully explained in lay-
men's terms and its benefits spelled out.

"The advertisement tells the consumer in understandable language
about the scanning system and its function. However, we need much
more promotional material of this type directed at the consumer,"
he said.

When FMI members ask about IBM's scanning equipment and service,
Aders said they, "give you very high marks." The only serious
complaint about the scanning equipment he noted, was in the area of
the standard display panel on the checkout unit.

"In tnis regard, I was told the brightness, size and orientation

more

Figure 5-5 *(Continued)*

111

```
                                                        Aders /IBM
                                                        Page Three


   were not visable enough for the consumer.   The checker can see it,

   but not the customer," he said.

        "This suggests," he noted, "that you have been worrying too much

   about us (the grocer) and not enough about our customers."

        Aders closed his talk by saying that, "keeping in touch with

   your (IBM) customer's needs and our (grocer) customer's needs is

   paramount.

        "Grocers know only too well that today it's not enough to simply

   sell the product.  Food retailing involves community activity, social

   concern and nutritional knowledge.  Our product must be packaged in

   concern for our customers' health and welfare.  I think your product

   might well be packaged in the same way," he said.


                                    ####
```

Figure 5-5 *(Continued)*

The First Paragraph

As you've heard before, many releases are read only through the headline and perhaps the first paragraph or two before the editor decides whether or not to run it.   That's why we've spent so much time talking about the headline, and why the first paragraph of the body copy merits special treatment and attention.

The first step toward getting your release accepted is to keep it from getting rejected, and this observation is not as obvious as it may seem at first glance.   Many releases are rejected on the basis of a simple downfall: failure to include any *news* in the first paragraph.

In fact, it's a good practice to put the most newsworthy information you have in the very first sentence and, if possible, to follow up with another relevant, newsworthy item in the second or third sentence.

The who, what, when, where, why, and how of your story should all be a part of this first sentence or two. For example:

> XYZ Corporation of Cityname, State has announced a revolutionary new light bulb capable of producing ten times the amount of light of an ordinary bulb at the same power, or as much light as an ordinary light bulb with only one-tenth the power consumption of standard light bulbs. The announcement came during a special Conference on Energy meeting in Washington, D.C. In addition to its extraordinary energy efficiency, this new light bulb boasts an average service life of fifteen years, and is planned to sell at a manufacturers' suggested U.S. resale price of only twenty cents. This new light bulb is the result of an intensive decade-long research and development effort by XYZ Corporation, an industry leader in lighting products.

The when of this and most releases would be specified by the date at the top of the page. This particular example contains two wheres: both the city and state of the company and the location of the Washington energy conference. The why of this and many good releases is the stated benefit or benefits the user will derive as a result of the announced news. And the how, which is implied in the phrase "revolutionary, new" is expressed in the last sentence.

This paragraph alone communicates the essential high points of this announcement, and for good reason. On radio, there isn't time for much more than the information in the first praagraph. In print, there may not be space for much more (depending on the importance of the news to each particular audience or readership).

There are two stylistic formats you should be aware of. First, all numbers have been spelled out. This is a safeguard against typographical or typing errors, since a missed keystroke would result in only a misspelled number instead of a wrong number. Second, the price is specified as the "manufacturers' suggested U.S. resale price." This recognizes the dealer's prerogative to set prices (anything else could fall under the forbidden category of "price fixing"). Also, the price in other countries may differ for reasons of currency exchange rates and different methods of distribution. This is a selling price to the end user, not a price to distributors and dealers (who, after all, have profit requirements of their own).

Now is a good time to review some of the examples of professionally prepared press releases we've enclosed.   Look at the way their opening paragraphs are written.   Can you observe any similarities?   Or draw any conclusions from their approach to the how-to-write-the-first-paragraph problem?   Do you agree with the way they're written? Disagree? Why?

You'll probably discover that this business of writing releases is easier than you expected.

Collapsible Copy

The first paragraph should always include the key points of a release. In the press for time in broadcasting and space in publishing, there may not be time or space for more.   You will want to be careful how you order the information in subsequent paragraphs, for much the same reason.   What's the *next* most important thing you'd like to see appear?   Place this next in the release, and follow this discipline as you write.

This is not to suggest that editors simply "lop off" whatever won't fit, though this may occasionally happen.   Rather, the editor may or may not be aware of the relative strengths and importance of the details.   Lacking any better indicator, an editor may decide that the sequence communicates the relative importance of the elements.

This tendency suggests that you compose the text of your release with what is called *collapsible copy*.   In rough terms, collapsible copy will read well from its beginning to the end of any given paragraph. This is a tremendous expedient for editors, enabling them to fit a release into an available space, which as often as not means more space for your story than it might have received if it required a more troublesome rewrite.

The Last Paragraph

The last paragraph of any release you write or have written for you should closely resemble the last paragraph of every other release you write or have written for you. This is the "for additional information" paragraph, and will read something like this:

>   For additional information about the (subject of this
> release)   and other   (related subject)   products   (or

News from │Sears│

FOR FURTHER INFORMATION:

Richard G. Williford
Dept. 703 - Public Relations
SEARS, ROEBUCK AND CO.
Sears Tower
Chicago, Illinois 60684
(312) 875-8313, 8325

The glamorous, super-competitive sport of international auto racing is the subject of the latest motion picture from Sears, Roebuck and Co.

Racing entrepreneur, Roger Penske, the sport's "man for all seasons," is the subject of an exciting 25-minute, 16-mm, color film titled "VROOM at the Top" that is available on a free loan basis.

"VROOM" highlights the activities of Penske's racing team, as typified by his entries in three of the world's most prestigious races -- Indianapolis 500, Monaco Grand Prix and the "World 600"-mile stock car race -- all on the same afternoon.

The film takes the viewer to the Indy spectacle, puts him in Penske's Grand Prix car for a behind-the-wheel view of the race course through the picturesque streets of Monte Carlo, and visits the world's longest stock car race at the Charlotte, N.C. Motor Speedway. It gives the auto racing fan a perspective of what is required, in terms of manpower, equipment, financing and preparation, to field a competitive racing team.

Here is an inside look at Penske's most ambitious racing effort yet: building an international racing team to compete in USAC, NASCAR and Grand Prix events with such talented drivers as Mario Andretti, Bobby Allison, Tom Sneva and John Watson.

-more-

F51144

Figure 5-6.   An excellent example of collapsible copy.   (Courtesy Sears, Roebuck & Co.)

VROOM traces Roger Penske's unique rise to success in both the auto
racing and business worlds, providing insight into Penske and a close-up,
behind-the-scenes look at his racing team in this fast-paced film.

"VROOM at the Top" includes a reprise of Roger's own race driving
achievements, as well as many of those of the late Mark Donohue, and
a recap of memorable moments of the famous Can-Am road racing series.

Penske's finely tuned supervision of his race shop and team, and
how it's turned into winning ways can be seen. Roger is portrayed as
a "doer" -- the complete executive and team manager -- not just a planner
or absentee car owner.

VROOM provides insight into the growing Penske empire, one that
stresses professionalism in the form of attitude, dedication and
attention to detail, and offers opportunity to those willing to
embrace these career traits. It shows how Penske uses his reputation
and determination as a former top driver, and now a successful corporate
head, to enhance the image and growth of his dynamic firm.

"VROOM at the Top" is distributed by Association Films' regional
libraries on a free-loan basis. Write Association Films, 866 Third
Avenue, New York, N.Y. 10022.

# # #

Figure 5-6 *(Continued)*

services), contact (name of contact) at (company name and mailing address); or phone (area code and phone number), (days of the week), between the hours of (hours when available).

If you have a teletypewriter on the TWX or Telex networks, include its access code and number information as well. Some companies use WATS (toll-free 800 numbers) for customer inquiries or permit collect calls. Again, include all the get-in-touch information you can.

Also, you may accept telephone orders via credit cards. In this case, add something like that shown below, keeping it newsy, not commercial.

Credit card orders are being accepted by phone at (the appropriate number); (Visa, Master Card, Carte Blanche, Diners Club, American Express, or whatever cards you honor should be listed here) will be honored.

You then need to mark the end of copy. Traditionally this is done either with three to five asterisks or with the number 30 surrounded by hyphens. Use either but not both. Both are shown below.

*****   --30--

6

Photographs

Can you describe a shovel? A wheelbarrow? A hairdo? A computerized dashboard? A new fabric?

Eventually, you could probably describe all of these in words, but photography provides a shorter, simpler, more direct way to communicate essentially visual information. And photos, especially good photos, tend to be more memorable than words.

This chapter will tell you how to take good press release photos. Even more important, you'll learn some of the tricks of planning for effective publicity photos. There's an easy formula for getting good "workhorse" photos taken, but there are also simple and effective ways to add pizzazz and sparkle—not just for effect's sake, but for effectiveness's sake—to make your photos even more memorable, and to give them a better chance of being selected by an editor. However, you should remember that though it costs more money to use a pro, the difference in quality usually means a better chance of a release running, justifying the expenditure.

Technical Insight

Before we discuss setting up a shot or a session, let's look briefly at the technical nuts-and-bolts magic that puts a picture into print. We'll see how the method by which a photo is reproduced affects the way it should be taken. (This is one of those sections you may want to skip now and pick up on later.)

You'll need a magnifying glass for this. If you flip ahead a few pages, you'll see some actual black-and-white publicity photos. Some were released by Sears, Roebuck & Company, others by Motorola Incorporated Semiconductor Group, some by the Food Marketing Institute. All are reproduced here with the permission of these organizations, for which we would like to thank them.

These photos were reproduced and circulated as 8" x 10" black and white glossy photographic prints, usually called 8" x 10" glossies for short. "Glossy" refers to the smooth finish on the surface of these photographic prints, and many of the snapshots you take are likely to be printed as glossies. Generally, snapshots that are not glossies have a matte finish. This is not as smooth, and is characterized by some surface texturing, often in a miniature cobblestone or beehive pattern.

Your snapshots, like these glossies, are printed on special photosensitive paper that's designed to darken where light strikes and remain white where light does not strike. Such papers offer a large range of intermediate shades of gray between the blackest black and the whitest white. Also, these shades of black, white, and gray flow into each other with a smooth, soft transition between subtle shades. For these reasons, photographic prints are referred to as "continuous tone."

Now use your magnifying glass to examine the pictures in this book. You'll find that while they look very much like continuous tone photos at first glance, they are really made up of thousands of little dots. There's only one shade of black, and it's the same black ink used to print the words on this page; the only shade of white is the white of the paper beneath.

If you're very observant, you'll have noticed that the little black dots are different sizes, and the larger the dot, the darker the apparent shade of gray.

The process begins when a photograph is covered with a special film, opaque except for an intricate pattern of transparent "dots." This film is called a "screen," and is usually specified by the number of lines (rows of dots) per inch. Most books and magazines use screens providing between 60 and 150 lines ("per inch" is implied).

Next, a special high-contrast film (with black and white, but no gray) is exposed. The film reacts to light in such a way that the more light striking an area, the more the dot in the area grows (within limits), which explains the different dot sizes when the picture is printed.

Finally, the high-contrast image is transferred to a metal plate treated with special chemicals. The plate is dipped in an acid bath which eats away the white areas, leaving the blacks raised, like a rubber stamp, to impress ink on paper.

While many newer processes have supplanted several of these traditional steps, the overall effect is the same.

The higher the contrast, the more pronounced the full blacks and whites and the fewer the number of shades of gray.   High contrast photographs reproduce extremely well, but at the expense of detail, which those missing intermediate shades of gray help define. Striking the right balance between contrast and detail always involves compromising one at the expense of the other.

The coarseness of the dot screen becomes an important consideration in this compromise.   While many magazines offer as fine a screen as 144 lines, many offer between 100 and 120 (their choice, not yours). Newspapers are generally even coarser, offering between 60 and 100 lines. The coarser the line screen, the more detail lost.

Also, while you'll probably be providing either 5" x 7" or 8" x 10" photographic prints, these may shrink down to as small as a single column's width—about two inches—again meaning a tremendous loss of detail.

It's important to take some steps in advance to ensure that your beautiful photo doesn't turn into a beastly square splotch.   Besides, if an editor thinks your pictures are likely to reproduce poorly, entire releases are likely to get rejected.

But it's easy enough to bring everything into focus, develop an approach that overcomes the negatives, and bring a few tricks of the trade into the picture.

Details, Details

Take a good look at what you have to photograph.   How big is it? Look at some of the details that will be in the picture.   Which are important?   If any were to be lost in the translation, obscured one way or another by the time the picture is printed, how much of a disadvantage would it be?   You'll have to start thinking about these things well before the photo is actually taken.

You may decide, after due consideration, that the detail is more important to communicate than the overall item.   For example, if you manufacture cars and are preparing a release about a new dashboard that displays printed messages in lights, you may want to take a close-up of a message being displayed instead of the whole car or whole dashboard.   If so, consider taking a close-up of the detail instead of a picture of the entire product.   There are two alternate techniques for this: the use of an *inset* and the use of a *graphic prop*.

An inset is a picture within a picture.   You could take either a close-up of the detail and inset the whole product, or take a picture of the whole product and inset a picture of the detail. The difference is in emphasis, of course, and the choice depends on the emphasis appropriate to your release.

A graphic prop involves using a photo or drawing of the detail, blown up to many times its actual size, as a background for the whole object in a photo. If you are, for example, offering a pocket calculator with unique new functions that are well-represented by a close-up of a few keys on the keyboard, you can have these blown up. (Sometimes this can be done with special lighting and a rear-screen projected slide.) When taking the photo of the calculator, the close-up is used as a background. The relevant special keys are kept clearly visible, of course.

A third alternative is somewhat more difficult to accomplish, and the services of a skilled professional photographer are strongly recommended. This technique involves a double exposure, most often composed in the darkroom by superimposing two images on top of each other. Since the need for detail in a double exposure is usually even more critical than usual, this technique should be used sparingly and quickly abandoned if there is any doubt of the clarity of the printed results. In many cases, however, the size and clarity of the details will be sufficiently adequate with a simple photograph of the whole unit showing them to good advantage.

Now we'll look at some ways you can give the look of your subject a boost. If your product is bone white, you wouldn't shoot it in the middle of a snowdrift, since white-on-white makes your product hard to discern from the background. If your product is black as soot, you wouldn't shoot it atop a bin of coal for the same reason; yet a surprising number of dark products are photographed against dark backgrounds, and light products against light backgrounds.

There's another mistake that's even more common: A great many backgrounds end up to be the same shade of gray as the product when photographed in black and white. But how can you tell before? You see in full "living" color, after all, and not in black and white—or do you?

There are a few simple tricks you can perform to "eyeball" the gray scale values of your product versus any given background. But learning them means another session (hopefully a brief one) of our science class.

Your eyes have two different kinds of light-sensitive sensors, called *rods* and *cones*. Cones are sensitive to colors, but require more light; rods require only a minimal amount of light, but are insensitive to differences in color. Together, these two types of sensors provide the normal vision you use for such things as reading this book, watching television, and performing normal daytime or nighttime activities.

(Rods give you night vision, the ability to make out shapes in near-total darkness.)

So one way to judge gray scales is to turn out all or most of the lights. If your blue doodad starts to blend into the red paper you've chosen to put behind it (or whatever the colors and materials are), make another selection and try again. After you've gained some experience, you'll learn to judge these gray scale effects with the lights on. Another version of this method is to squint, shutting out most of the light that normally reaches your eyes. The effect is similar to that outlined above.

Still another trick is to view the scene through colored filters. Dark gray is the best choice, since less neutral colors tend to favor certain colors and disfavor others. But if you find one item (either subject or background) dark and the other light through *both* a blue filter and a red one, the chances are good that you will have good gray scale compatibility.

There may be times you can't avoid using colors with the same gray scale. If these are indeed different colors, the photographer may be able to increase their gray scale contrast through the use of an appropriate color filter in front of the lens. One important instance of this inseparable foreground-background situation occurs when the foreground is a detail on your subject.

A particularly thorny color to photograph is, of course, gray, since it can appear to be nearly white or black when photographed. A product with a gray case surrounding a black panel, for example, will appear to have a white case and a dark gray panel if photographed against a black background, or a dark gray case with a black panel and gray lettering (assuming any panel lettering is originally white) if photographed against a white background. Colors would appear more close to natural if photographed against a yellow or salmon or light blue background.

Retouching and Make-Up

There are other techniques you can use to help show a detail to its best advantage. Primary among these are photographic retouching and the use of make-up, but not the kind you'll find at a cosmetics counter.

Depending on the amount of retouching you need, it may represent a minor investment or something on the order of ten times the cost of the photography. Retouching should only be attempted by experts;   if you're using a professional photographer, there may be   a retoucher he or she can recommend.

Make-up is a lot simpler to arrange and execute, and   the   fewer modifications you need to make after the photo is taken, the better off your photo and your budget will be.   Make-up can be as simple as a soft pencil and a bit of white paint applied with a fine brush by a skilled and steady hand.

One recurring problem, with everything becoming electronic, is a black switch on a black panel.   A bit of gray paint used as make-up to provide a thin outline along the edges of the switch will help make it more visible.

An automobile tire will benefit from black touch-up paint on the rubber and white touch-up paint on the lettering.   A textured surface that is otherwise unmarked (for example, glassware or pottery) can benefit either by the use of a pencil to help define edges, or a little graphite from the pencil rubbed onto the molded features.

How would you shoot a transparent dry cleaning overwrap bag? Depending on the requirements of your release, you could paint the back of it a color close to (but not quite) the color of your background to help define it.   Or you could separate it from your background by bringing it forward somewhat and lighting it primarily from behind. Another technique is to use *selective focus* and try to bring the bag into focus while bringing the background out of focus.   Of course, this depends on the background having enough detail to make it seen in focus.

But make-up isn't only used to correct the photographic short-comings of your subject.

Cosmetics

Take a big, thick, juicy steak, put it on a plate under some hot lights for an hour and you'll get a wonderful shot of dry meat.   But if you put some glycerin in a perfume atomizer and spray it on the steak, it'll still look moist and mouth-watering when the shutter finally clicks. (But don't eat the steak after the session.   If you don't know why, ask your mother about glycerin.)

Suppose that you're photographing something made of polished wood.   A little salad oil on a paper towel helps really bring out the shine.

And these are just two examples of how a few cosmetic touches can really make whatever you're shooting look its best.

If you're shooting screws and bolts, you may want to roll them in a graphite powder then blow or wipe them clean for a little extra sparkle and groove definition.   Or if you're shooting a phonograph record, a light coat of a thin liquid floor wax will help keep it from attracting dust while you set up and shoot.

Before you go off to the library to look up the last umpteen years of the Heloise column for more hints, talk with the engineers who helped design your product or subject, or with the photographer you plan to use. Between them, you'll uncover a bag of tricks to help you dress up your product. This isn't to suggest that you should make your photograph misleading, but rather that it should do its job of showing your product.

If you'll be working with food, the special services of a home economist are especially valuable. (Your photographer probably knows of one with studio experience.)   They know how to use a blowtorch to put grill marks on a steak, make vegetables look glamorous, pick out the off-color peas, add a little yellow food coloring to help the butter in the mashed potatoes show up, spritz the outside of a glass to help it look fresh and chilly, and do more nice things for the way food looks than anyone, short of a *cordon bleu* chef.

If you're working with clothing—especially if you're going to have models or mannequins wearing it—a professional dresser can help everything look its best.   They know how to pin or slit shirts and blouses to a trim and perfect fit. They know where a little steam, a little water, or a little ironing will help and where a little paper will help flatten an inappropriate bulge or how to coordinate outfits and accessories to look good on camera.

There are other experts you'll want to consider when you work with models, from hairdressers to cosmetics specialists.   In every case, try to use them, because the difference a professional can make is remarkable. And the same is true of the models themselves.   Your neighbor's kids may look cute, but take a look at a "head sheet" from a local model agency.   They're usually very happy to cooperate, and there's no charge to look at pictures of the models they represent. You'll appreciate the difference a professional can make.

But should you use a model?

When to Use a Model

Whatever the product or service you offer and no matter how inappropriate it may be to the release you've planned, somebody, sometime

Figure 6-1.   Here a model is used to help bring off a visual pun. The doodads on her sunhat are all solar- or light-related electronic products. (Courtesy Motorola Semiconductor Products Inc.)

Figure 6-2.   Here models are used in conjunction with graphic props to help give back-to-school clothes a fresh angle.   (Courtesy Sears, Roebuck & Co.)

is going to suggest that you use a picture of a young, pretty, scantily clad girl.   In most cases, don't.   It won't help your product and it won't impress the editor.   Indeed, it may infuriate a number of the people you're trying to impress, men and women alike.   There are times, however, when a model is appropriate.   You might well be selling cosmetics, lingerie, adult entertainment, or weight loss aids. Remember, though, your picture will get only a limited amount of space.   A person could draw attention from your product, but may be useful to show the product or service in use.   A model in the photo may also help give some idea of the size of your product, how it's used, who uses it, and where.   Ask yourself whether adding a person would make your photo more meaningful.   If so, then by all means consider it, trying always to keep your use of a model in context and appropriate.

Generally, you will consider using a model either to illustrate the benefits or the applications of a product.   This involves such details as costuming and deciding whether to shoot on location, where the product is normally used, or in the studio.   You'll have to consider the image of your models.   Should they look like "real people" in the midst of normal activities or should they look posed?

The answer to both questions is in the reason you decided to use a model in the first place.   If the model is there to give an idea of size or proportion or to demonstrate the actual conditions in which the subject of the photo is used, you want the photo to look natural.   You can accomplish this best by showing the model using the product.   Try selecting one small instant of use and posing the model to it—and try to avoid "look at the camera and say cheese" type of poses.

One final word: Hold off using models at all until you've had at least several months of publicity experience.   The use of models adds expense and complications to a photo session, and while you may want to jump into publicity feet first, you'll have plenty of demanding details to attend to in the beginning.

Tabletoppers

The simplest type of publicity shot is also the one you'll probably use most often.   Here, the subject of your photo is placed against a neutral background and photographed close up enough to fill the photo.   This type of photo is generally called a *tabletopper,* and it's generally shot on a special photographic stand called a *sweep table.*

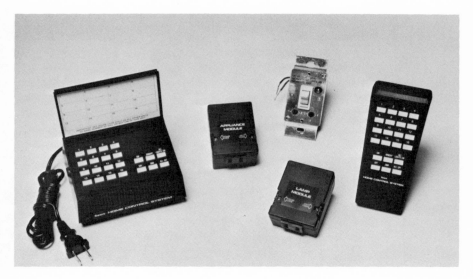

A

B

Figure 6-3A&B.   Product groupings arranged as tabletoppers. (A. Courtesy Sears, Roebuck & Co., B. Courtesy Radio Shack)

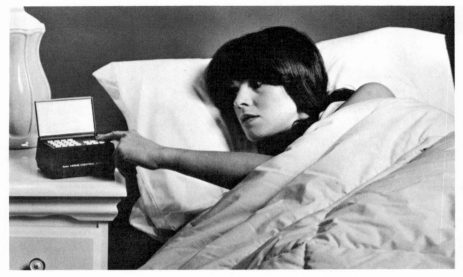

C

D

Figure 6-3C&D. The same products are seen here in an application shot. (C. Courtesy Sears, Roebuck & Co., D. Courtesy Radio Shack)

A sweep table offers a flat horizontal surface that curves upward into a flat vertical background, and curves downward into a disappearing foreground.   The result is one continuous surface that "sweeps" upward from foreground to background, with enough horizontal surface in the midground to let you set up a product.   A regular table, by comparison, is discontinuous, and would present both a forward edge and a back edge (or corner if it's backed up to a wall).

Some sweep tables are made of white, translucent plastic, which provides the photographer with the option of lighting the subject softly from behind or beneath.   More usually, though, a roll of wide seamless paper of a selected color, including many metallic and special effect finishes, is hung on a bracket above the back of the sweep table. The subject is then photographed with the seamless paper as a background.   The proper selection of a background, as discussed in the beginning of the chapter, can help enhance the appearance of your subject.

Some tabletoppers are extremely simple.   After selecting the appropriate background, positioning the subject to its best advantage, and balancing the lighting levels, you're ready to shoot.   These generally result in a simple portrait of an inanimate object, called a "product shot."   There's nothing wrong with simple product shots; they form the bulk of the population of all publicity photos.   They're relatively easy and inexpensive to execute, and even the less expensive professional photographers perform admirably in taking them.

One step up from the simple product shot is the prop shot.   Like product shots, most prop shots are tabletoppers, meaning relatively simple and inexpensive set-up and execution of your photo.

Prop pictures can give a very good idea of size.   The term "prop," short for property, originated in the theater.   It refers to any small thing or device that contributes to the storytelling.   Props serve much the same function in photography.   A pencil next to a small calculator helps contribute to the "story" of the calculator in two ways.   First, it provides the contrast between the old way and the new way of performing calculations, and second, it helps one appreciate the size of the calculator compared to the pencil.   This automatic understanding of the size of an unfamiliar item from seeing it in proportion to a familiar item is called "scaling."

If scaling is the fundamental reason for your decision to use a prop, there are some obvious suggestions, including rulers, yardsticks, pinheads, someone's hand, or, for that matter, any other relevant part of a body, a car, and a football field.   But the obvious is not as good a choice as the not-so-obvious.   Just as we've seen how a little twist can attract an editor's attention in writing the who-what-when-where-why-how of a release, the same holds true for pictures.

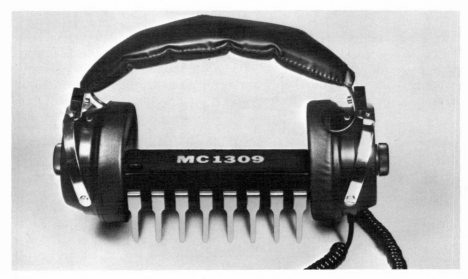

A

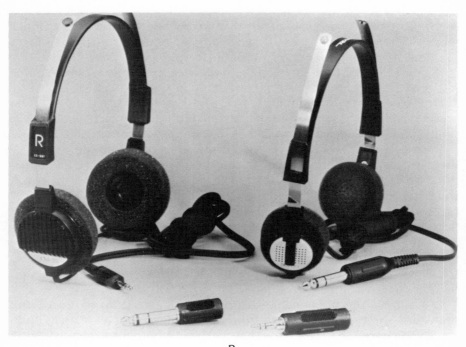

B

Figure 6-4A&B&C. Excellent tabletoppers. Note the imaginative use of head-phones as props. (A. Courtesy Motorola Semiconductor Products Inc., B & C Courtesy Radio Shack)

C

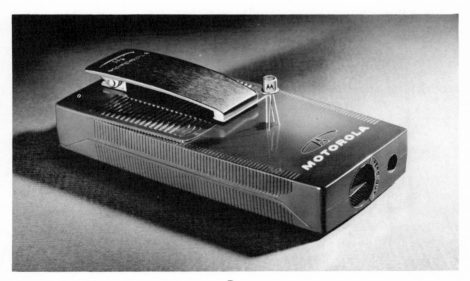

D

Figure 6-4D. A tiny transistor atop a pocket pager that incorporates it. (Courtesy Motorola Semiconductor Products Inc.)

Visual puns are one easy way to accomplish this twist.   If your product is metal pipe, you might want to pose a short length of it with a rack of smoking pipes, a bowl of tobacco, and a large ash tray.   If your product is house paint, you might show a few paint cans, brushes, and rollers posed with a fine art painting.   If you're showing pool tables, you can set up a lifeguard station with a lifeguard.   If your product is eyeglasses, pose them with an array of drinking glasses. Borrow a few (hopefully, controllable) birds from a local pet shop to pose with badminton birdies if they're your product.   For slide projectors, place one at the bottom of a playground slide.   The only rules is not to be confusing.   Always make it obvious which is the feature product, which are the props.   This can be done by careful composition and cropping.

Some editors enjoy corny shots more than others, and this kind of shot can definitely be considered corny.   Still, the visual pun is usually a better approach than a straight tabletop product shot.   Just exercise some taste and control to make sure the props don't detract from the primary purpose of the shot: showcasing your product.   The easiest way to achieve this compromise is to keep the props simple and mi- nimal, and to mix the visual pun with other approaches.

An approach with fewer pitfalls is choosing a prop that indirectly relates to the product being photographed.   For example, two decades ago the news was full of stories of spies using tiny transmitters dis- guised as martini olives.   Some manufacturers of transistors were successful in getting photographs of their new devices into newspaper business pages when they posed them next to olives or filled martini glasses with them.

If your product is a cardiac pacemaker, you can pose it next to a heart-shaped box of Valentine's Day candy.   If your product is corn oil, you can use a few ears of corn or a motor oil pour spout.   Use an aquarium with a few small tropical fish in the background for fish- ing tackle.   Suntan lotion provides a fitting background for sunglasses, and a burning candle with a dimly lighted background helps showcase a light switch.

The same technique can be applied to services, which are often dif- ficult to portray pictorially.   A globe or world map shown with an array of travel folders can help a travel agency send its message with a picture.   Car keys, tools, and spark plugs identify an auto repair service.   White gloves or work gloves, a brush, and a dust pan with a pile of dust in it are fitting for a cleaning service.   A styrofoam snowman with a shovel in his hands can do the job for a snowplowing service.   And a wedding cake sawed neatly down the center and separated slightly can quite effectively communicate the idea of a marriage counseling service.

A

B

Figure 6-5A-D.   These four photos demonstrate the use of props to add interest to a photo. (Courtesy Sears, Roebuck & Co.)

C

D

Another significant way in which photography can include props is the *application shot*, which actually shows the product in use.

One type of application shot is done with a tabletop. A few items are placed on a level surface without the need for a special location, and the props can either provide an actual demonstration of the product in use, or merely symbolize it.   If the product is a swizzle stick, for example, placing it in a glass provides an application shot. If the product is kitty litter, you might want to show a bag of it next to a little box that contains some of it.   If the product is a ballpoint pen, you can place it atop a written note, doodles, or written calculations.   If the product is dog food, you can use a dog dish, a leash, a dog toy, or a dog in an application shot.   If the product is a classical record or sheet music, you can place an appropriate musical instrument nearby.

Another type of application shot shows the product in use.   This usually requires that the photographer go on location or that a surrogate location be set up at the photographer's studio.   If the product is a complex piece of medical equipment, it's virtually mandatory that an application shot be taken at a hospital or medical laboratory. The only application location suitable for a race car is a race track. Cooking utensils, on the other hand, may be shot in virtually any kitchen, including a dummy   kitchen that the photographer sets up or has available in his studio.   The same kitchen setting may be suitable for glamorous shots of foods being prepared, if a food is your product.   If you sell tools to the construction trades, you'll probably have to visit a construction site to get the right ambience for   an application shot.

Patterns

Another approach to adding pizzazz to your pictures is to look for either bold or recurring geometric patterns, and arrange for a *good* photographer to shoot them.   If you have a bottling plant, he may find an unusual and artistic angle from which to shoot the bottles, using one more of the tricks in his bag, for an extremely attractive shot.   Editors like to dress up a dull page, even when they don't run the accompanying story, and it's also not unusual for this kind of shot, if available in color, to be requested for a trade magazine or cover photo.   If you manufacture gun barrels, the photographer may shoot down the middle, showing the rifling grooves inside.   If you have any kind of production line or open stock area, you can usually find attractive patterns within them.

Other Approaches

A variation on this theme involves pictures not usually seen by the human eye.   A microscopic, infrared, ultraviolet, or X-ray view of your product, or some component part of it, can be both attractive and intriguing. If you manufacture dolls with mechanical or electrical parts inside, an X-ray can provide a memorable shot. ("What makes baby run?")   If you sell insulation, an infrared photo showing where heat escapes, possibly a before-and-after set of photos, can be a dramatic and graphic demonstration of your product's benefits, as well as a timely and topical addition to an editor's page.   If you manufacture oil filters, cigarette filters, air filters, furnace filters, or water treatment filters, a microscopic view of the structure of the material you use draws attention and adds credibility to your product.

Another approach to both photography and the release itself is to promote your product indirectly.   For example, if you sell or manufacture something that has been recently written up or reported in a book or major publication, issue a release (with the cooperation and prior approval of the publisher) describing both the coverage and the product.   Include a photo showing the product and the publication together.   Use an actual product, not just any photo that might appear in the book.   Since it's unusual to see most products appearing next to books or magazines, you'll at least get the editor's attention. And again, the unusual can outpull the usual.

Personnel Photos

One type of photo that you never want to be too imaginative with is the personal portrait, a very formal photograph of each of the key people in your organization.   One of your first publicity activities will be to arrange for a file of "stock" photos of top and upcoming personnel.   Later, when they're quoted in a release, you'll want to include a photo.   Since the topmost people in an organization are usually the busiest and least available, having a picture on hand may be the only way you can include one with the release and still get it out while its information is timely.   And remember, the more people you involve in the photo sessions (within reason), the more reasonable your cost-per-photo is likely to be.

The reason for choosing upcoming people is that they're the most likely to be promoted, and promotions to key positions in your company are great ways to get coverage.   Editors, including photo editors, are usually on the lookout for pictures of key people, the more prominent the better. Photos are kept on hand in a photo file, an indexed library of file photos used when people say or do something interesting. You don't need a release to go with this kind of photo, either. Simply send the photo with a short caption identifying the individual and the position with your company. You should also include some brief biographical information, where-to-be-reached data, whom to contact at your company for additional information, and perhaps a one-sentence description of what your company does. Include a note which says something like:

Dear editor,

This photo is being sent to you for your files and for use as needed. If we can be of any further assistance, please contact me.

Just as photo editors appreciate file photos of key personnel, they also respond favorably to file photos of business locations (especially those of manufacturers, but also to those of other businesses). Again, a professional with experience in taking "architectural" photos can be worth the extra money. Depending on the size and scope of your operations, you will have to decide how many of your locations to have photographed. In each case, identify the facility, the specific activity there, its affiliation with your company (branch, wholly-owned division, satellite operation, etc.), its exact location, and pertinent statistics (like number of employees, square footage area, when constructed or when you assumed occupancy), and where to go for additional information. The note above is also suitable as a cover letter for this mailing.

One additional comment: Whenever you go to the trouble and expense of hiring a good photographer for either a "stock," or file, photo or for an important announcement, carefully investigate the usually minimal additional expense of having the shot taken in color as well as black and white. While you may never print any given color shot, there are times when you may be asked if color photography is available. These times are usually unique opportunities for excellent coverage. They may include magazine covers, special feature articles, books, or the incorporation of your photos (often with a photo credit to your company) in a brochure, annual report, or ad. Your own advertising program can also take advantage of the photography you shoot for publicity purposes.

Planning the Session

There's a simple sequence of events you'll want to follow in preparing for your photo session.

1. Decide what you want the photo to accomplish.

Are you announcing a new product?   A new application for an existing product?   Are you keying in on a specific feature or benefit? Are readers or viewers familiar with this type of product?   Does yours look somehow different?   Is there something that distinguishes yours from the others?

Take a good, long look at what you want your release to accomplish, then consider how photography can help get the job done.   We've already discussed the major categories under which a photo might fall, and seen how they can work.   Are any of them helpful?   Don't get needlessly or inappropriately fancy, and don't make your shot so cluttered that you can't tell the subject from the props, but do what you can to add to the effectiveness of what you're trying to accomplish.

2. Give yourself at least three choices of shots.

Once you've decided what you want your release to accomplish, you will need to consider how you will use photography to help accomplish it.   It may seem tedious on first consideration, but the best approach to this decision is to make a lengthy list of all your options, methodically eliminating those that are too complex, too expensive, not striking enough, and so on.   Leave yourself at least three of your best options.

3. Sketch your ideas.

Don't worry about your artistic talents.   You need only deal in rough approximations of overall shapes—circles, cylinders, boxes, rectangles, and so on.   The roughest of sketches will convey what goes where, and you can help by jotting down names or labels, or numbering items and attaching a list of what corresponds to each number.   The sketches you make will give you a better feeling of what the eventual photo will look like.

If details are important, try roughly sketching them in as well. If it's hard to make them out in a sketch, it will probably be hard to make them out in a printed photo.   Don't be bashful about trying a given sketch several times until everything "fits."   It may help you to work with a few props while you're sketching, adjusting their positions or your point of view for the best perspective, and as a double-check on proportions.   It's a lot less expensive to go through these "fidgets" in the comfort of your office than it would be to do the same thing at the photographer's studio, where you are charged for time in addition to materials.

4. Select a photographer.

Virtually every population center in the world has a full-time or part-time professional photographer, and most have a great many. Those who specialize in weddings, school yearbooks, and class portraits probably aren't your best choices for publicity photos.   Specialists in photos for advertising and graphic arts are the cream of the crop, and your best choice if you can afford them.   In the middle are those who generally specialize in photography full time for a newspaper or institution, and who freelance by taking publicity and product photos to supplement their incomes.

In each case, don't make a selection until you've seen samples of a photographer's work and understand the photographer's rates. Most have compiled a portfolio of their best work and will be happy to give you an opportunity to review it and discuss their facilities, capabilities, and rates.

When you review their portfolios, look for good composition. Will everything still "read" when the photo is reproduced in ink, only a column or two in width?   Good contrast (fully black blacks, strong whites, and well-defined differences between the grays) and good lighting (are parts of what you see in each picture disappearing unintentionally into too-dim or too-bright regions?) are also important.   As you inspect each photo, make notes either during the review or immediately afterward.   Maybe you'll find a rising star; a young photographer not yet charging an arm and a leg who still offers professional results.

While you're likely to find one photographer you'll want to use most of the time, have one or two alternate choices available for those inevitable situations when you can't get your session scheduled when you need it.

5. Schedule your session.

Now that you've determined the who, what, why, and how of your photo, it's time to determine the when and where.   Are special locations or facilities required?   Arrangements will have to be made.   Will you need special props or people (including models)?   You'll need time to make these arrangements, too.

Talk the *shooting* over with your photographer.   Review your sketches.   Make sure you both understand all the requirements.   Get an idea of how long it will take to set up, how long it will take to light, and how long it will take to shoot.   Know how long it will take to make all the other necessary arrangements.   Then set a date and time that will permit you to take all the necessary preparatory steps and permit the photographer to devote the time the session requires to you.

6. Finalize the arrangements!

Begin by making yourself a checklist.   Are the products and props you need ready for shooting?   Who will get them ready for you?   Can you arrange for duplicates in case something happens to something?

Are the people you need available?   Will you need models?   Have you and the photographer made your selections?   Talked to the agency?   To the models?   How about dressers and stylists?   Home economists?

Are special equipment operators needed?   Or special equipment (for example, a power supply to light up the panel of a non-functional "dummy" of an electronic product that is not yet in production)?

Will you need a graphic prop?   Who will prepare it?   When?   Is it possible to have a duplicate prepared—just in case?

When you're satisfied that you've identified all the arrangements, all the items, and all the people you'll need, methodically arrange for, confirm, and reconfirm everything.

7. Be at the session.

Photographers, especially professional photographers, are capable of managing all of the technical aspects of your session, but *you* have to be the expert when it comes to what you want the shot to accomplish and what's important to the shot.   The camera's viewfinder will give you an idea of what your shot will look like, or the photographer may be able to take a Polaroid that'll show you right there and then how your picture will look.

This is the time to be reasonably critical and finicky.   Make sure you get the photo the way you want it, but don't overdo it or you may find the photographer less than cooperative the next time.

After the Session

Even once your session is over, your involvement with it won't be. Photographers generally shoot any given set-up several times, with variations in lighting or exposure.   There may also be minor variations in the set-up, made as you go along.   As a result, there will be a number of photos from which you will have to make your selection.   These are usually provided on a *proof sheet* (also called a *contact sheet* or *contact print*).   This is a single piece of photographic paper on which a number of photos appear;   it's made by placing the strip of exposed and developed film negatives on top of the photographic paper under a piece of glass, then exposing the paper with a brief light to print the negatives' actual size.

Give yourself a head start by picking the best shot or two on the sheet.   Pay attention to the contrast, the exposure (is it too light or too dark overall?), and the details.   The photographer can make some minor corrections in printing your blow-ups.

Show your selections to the photographer, and share your comments.   Tell what you like about the shots you've selected, and what your reservations are about details that might or might not come out as well as you'd hoped.   The photographer may be able to make some small corrections in the darkroom when preparing the enlargements of the shots you've selected.

The enlargement should be the same size as the photos you want to provide for your releases: 5" x 7" is a practical minimum; 8" x 10" is preferred.   The only exception to this is if you have planned and budgeted for extensive retouching, in which case the retoucher will want to work with as large a print as possible, requiring a *copy stand* shot later, in which a picture of the picture is taken.

Once the actual-size master print is ready, it's time to find a way to get your copies made.

Quantity Photo Prints

If you deal with less than about twenty names on your whole publicity list, you might or might not find your photographer willing to make the extra prints you need for a reasonable price.   Most lists, however, are larger, and most one-at-a-time reproduction costs are prohibitively expensive.

Fortunately, there is an attractive alternative available—businesses that specifically provide quantity prints from your original photo. A same-size negative is made of your original print; this is then used to sequentially print whatever number of photos are required. Often, these are printed on a continuous roll of paper and processed by machine, finally being trimmed at the end of processing into the flat, rectangular shape you're used to seeing.

Generally, the cost of a quantity print is a fraction of the price of duplicate prints from a photographer—somewhere between half and a twentieth!   The fraction depends, of course, on how expensive the photographer's charges are, how inexpensive the quantity printer's charges are, and how many copies you need.

The quantity photo printer, you understand, is not a printer in the conventional printing-press-and-ink sense, and you should never ask a printer to give you quantity reproductions of your photo. What you're likely to get is a photo with a built-in dot screen, printed as ink on conventional paper.   When a publication tries to reproduce this (if they *do* try—most know better and just decide not to run the picture, meaning the release is likely to accompany it on a one-way trip to the trash), the publication's own dot screen will interfere with the repro-duction's dot screen, resulting in a geometric "interference" pattern overshadowing the picture.

Controlling Costs

We have reviewed most of the areas where you will be incurring ex-penses in taking and making the photos to go with your releases. Let's take another look at these areas to see where we can economize. Some things that increase expenses, and should be avoided, if possible, are:

Models

Dressers

Hairdressers

Home economists

Shooting on location

Retouching

Some ways to reduce expenses include:

Keeping shots simple

Shooting more than one set-up at a time

Releasing 5" x 7" prints instead of 8" x 10" prints

And you're sure to work up a few short-cuts of your own. If you're a skilled amateur and can afford the time, you may want to try duplicating what the professionals do, eventually, and take the pictures yourself.   But you'd better be well-to-do because equipment can get expensive.   And you'd better be good at it, or your releases may suffer.

That's the Picture

This has been about as thorough a crash course in photography for publicity as you're likely to find, with one exception.   You'll learn this much or more when you get into it yourself, and probably even more rapidly.

7

Printing

Printing is one aspect of the problem of reproduction and distribution of releases. Type masters. Count names. Send stock and masters to printers and photos to quantity printers. Pull selected mailing labels. Pick up releases. Collate and staple releases. Pick up photos. Stuff envelopes with releases, photos, and cardboard stiffeners. Affix labels to envelopes. Seal envelopes. Affix postage to envelopes. Deliver to post office (or arrange for UPS pickup). Log each step. Prepare documentation for fulfillment packages. Prepare files for results. These are *some* of the details of printing. Let's see how to make it all simpler.

Copy Machine Printing

One of the easiest (and least desirable) ways of duplicating your releases is to stick them on your office copying machine. But unless it's a very expensive copier and you can't tell the difference between a copy and an original, you won't be putting your best foot forward. And if you're trying to copy a release typed on your letterhead onto the copy machine's usual paper, the look of your letterhead will suffer.

If your office copy machine is capable of making good copies on plain (untreated) paper, you may enjoy acceptable results by copying only the text part of the page and using your special news release letterhead as the plain paper onto which copies will be made. There are several techniques for providing the text only to be copied—all are called *mastering.*

One crude approach is to trim away the letterhead parts of the page, mounting the text portion that remains on a plain white sheet of paper with glue or rubber cement.   Another crude approach is to use white paint to mask off those portions of the page that include your letterhead.

A better approach is to know what area of the page on your letter-head is available for text, and to retype the text into that area of a plain white sheet of paper.   This kind of text-only master is usable both in duplicating a release onto news release letterhead in a plain paper office copier, and in duplicating a release onto news release letterhead in offset printing.   A similar text-portions-only technique can be used to cut masters for Gestetner (Ditto) and mimeograph machines.

As soon as the number of releases you need both for your mailing and for your own file copies exceeds 30 to 50 copies, you will want to consider any of these latter techniques strongly, since the cost of making copies on your office copy machine will soon grow prohibitive.

If you have already made the investment in, or have access to, an offset printing press, a Gestetner (Ditto), or a mimeograph machine, your decision on method may have been made for you.   If not, offset printing by an outside service is probably your best choice—for several reasons.

Offset Printing

Offset printing is a relatively simple printing process where a plate is used to transfer ink onto paper.   This printing plate is generated through basically photographic techniques from your one master copy of the text of the release.

There are two types of plates: *wet plates*, which are generally used for a press run of several hundred copies (or less) and then discarded, and *metal plates*, which may be used to run several thousand copies, removed from the printing press, and either recycled or stored for another run at a later time.   Wet plates, by the way, are sometimes also called *paper plates*.   Since most publicity releases are timely and seldom need to be reprinted, wet plates are usually the preferred choice for printing.   Often, on a lengthy run, depending on the printer you use, it will be less expensive to generate two or three wet plates than to generate a single metal plate, even if the metal plate is to be recycled.   Also, since more printers are capable of generating wet plates than are capable of generating metal plates on the premises, there is often a time savings involved in choosing wet plates.

If your letterhead is itself black ink, you can save a little money by preparing your master on letterhead and having your plates generated with the letterhead in place, and then printing onto plain paper. Otherwise, you'll have to preprint your news release letterhead, supply the printer with whatever quantity of stationery the run requires, make the plate from a text-only master, and print onto your prepared letterhead instead of plain paper. The advantage is that you won't be paying for paper for the run; the disadvantage is that you'll already have paid for the paper, and printed letterhead costs more than plain stock. By the way, black ink is definitely recommended for your releases.

Of course, if your letterhead includes any color that isn't black, you're much better off with a text-only master, printing onto preprinted letterhead news release stationery (see Chapter 5). You could print the additional colors on top of the release using a separate master, called a *separation*, for each portion that is in a different color. This takes more time, however, to run each color, and for drying between runs. It also costs more money, partly because it's a shorter run than would be involved in preparing blank stationery all at once.

With offset printing, you have a large choice of paper on which your release can be printed (or, for that matter, your letterhead). Different papers are different prices, for a variety of reasons. One is content, also called rag, which is a measure of the quality of the paper. One is thickness, usually specified with a term called weight, in numbers of pounds: "40 pound offset" is a good choice for releases. One is color, with extra costs usually associated with colors other than white, or with very white whites. Another is finish (you won't want a very slick, or shiny, finish for your releases). Also, at any moment in time, there's probably somebody on strike somewhere, making for short supplies of certain kinds of paper, or long deliveries, or extra costs. Talk with local printers before you make a selection. They can get you samples from the paper companies and provide some invaluable advice on your choices.

Finding Printers

While offset printing isn't the only method of printing available, it's usually the best choice for the requirements of most publicity programs. It's fast, fairly inexpensive, and well suited for quantities between about 50 and several thousand.

Offset printing equipment is also reasonably inexpensive as a capital equipment investment for a small business, so there are a number of small, independent offset printers almost anywhere in the world. Many of them have words like "quick," "speedy," or "instant" in their names. Ask your company purchasing agent. If that proves fruitless, the phone book is a good place to start looking. You'll probably find a surprising number of offset printers close to you.

The next step is to see who's best able to handle your work and who's got the best prices. The best way to do this is to issue a bid letter, spelling out what you're up to, what your needs are, and asking for a quote. In the example that follows, substitute the numbers that are appropriate for the publicity program you're planning.

Your company's name
Your company's address

Date

Printer's name
Printer's address

Dear sir or madam:

(Company name) is about to begin a publicity program that will require the regular printing of our news releases. We are asking you to enter a formal competitive bid according to the details presented in this letter. We will need your bid by (date).

While the specifics of quantity and number of pages will vary from release to release, quantities will average 150, and the average release will run two pages. For the purposes of your bid, please offer prices for 1-, 2-, and 3-page releases in quantities of 50, 100, 200, 300, and 500 (fifteen total bids). Assume that we will provide preprinted 8½" x 11" news release letterhead, with separate styles for first page and following pages.

When estimating, please specify your normal and worst-case turnaround time on each job.

Also specify which of the following services you offer, and what, if any, additional cost would be involved to include each service in each of the above (fifteen) quantities:

Collate and staple (for multiple-page releases)

Pick up and deliver

Rush service (specify turnaround time)

Separate into bundles of 20 or 50 (specify)

Our on-going program calls for preparing and printing 100 different news releases in the next twelve months. We are interested in establishing good relations with a prime source for our offset printing needs. We look forward to your timely response to this request for a bid, and ask you to enclose a few samples of your work.

If you have any questions, feel free to contact me.

Sincerely,

(signature)
Your name
Director of Public Relations

When you compile the results, pay attention to which of the extra services are available and to how quick a response you get, in addition to the raw numbers.   Also, calculate the cost per page for each of the fifteen examples (divide the cost by the number of copies, and divide this figure by the number of pages).   Since you've specified that two-page releases with a run of 150 are typical, beware of figures for this item on the bid sheet running lower per page than the other figures; this indicates an attempt to lead the bid, and unless the other figures are also lower overall, may be an attempt to put one over on you.

You'll want to keep all the bids you receive on file to provide yourself with quick access to a backup printing source in case something (like a vacation, a fire, a flood, a big job that ties up the shop) makes your first choice temporarily unavailable to you.

Mailing Labels

Every time you send out a batch of releases, there's also a batch of envelopes to which you'll have to affix the names and addresses of some portion of your publicity mailing list. If you issue 50 releases a year to an average of 100 names, that's 5,000 address labels to affix; if you issue 100 releases to an average of 750 names, that's 75,000 address labels to affix.

Obviously, unless you're on a shoestring budget and have time or people to spare, you're not about to address those envelopes by hand. There are a number of ways of preparing duplicate labels, including special purpose machines and computers, but one relatively recent development is the best method for most programs the size of the one you're likely to oversee.

There's a special variety of pressure-sensitive labels made to be run in place of sensitized paper in Xerox and certain other electrostatic office copying machines. These labels are available from Xerox, Avery, and possibly other sources.

In each box of labels is a special master sheet with lines in a special shade of light blue ink, called *non-repro blue*, that copy machines like the ones above can't pick up. These mark-off areas on the master correspond to the area of each label on the label sheets. Once you've typed your mailing list onto masters, as many copies as you need can be run off. Even if you don't have the right kind of copy machine, there are almost always small copy centers available to perform this service for a nominal charge (or your printer may offer this service).

Assuming everything is properly aligned (there are instructions with the labels), the individual labels will peel off of the backing paper one at a time, and with their pressure sensitive, sticky backing, can be placed directly on the envelopes.

Other Printing

Releases and stationery aren't the only things you'll need printed in order to get your publicity job done.

If you get involved in a press conference or media event, you'll need to prepare invitations. If you need to prepare a release package or press kit, you'll need a jacket to package the materials, which you may or may not want to preprint with distinctive corporate identification. You may also need business cards. And you may want to generate some special forms for your own internal use to keep track of things. And when those inquiries come in, you'll need to prepare any number of materials for a fulfillment package, including dealer lists, price sheets, product information sheets, catalogs, or whatever is appropriate to your business. Even if many of these materials are supplied by manufacturers whose products you offer, you will probably want to overprint these materials with your own company's name, address, and phone number.

By now, you've been introduced to all the techniques you need to prepare a layout, have a design prepared, find and select a printer, control your costs, and get the job done. Which, you'll have to admit, is a lot you didn't know about before we got started.

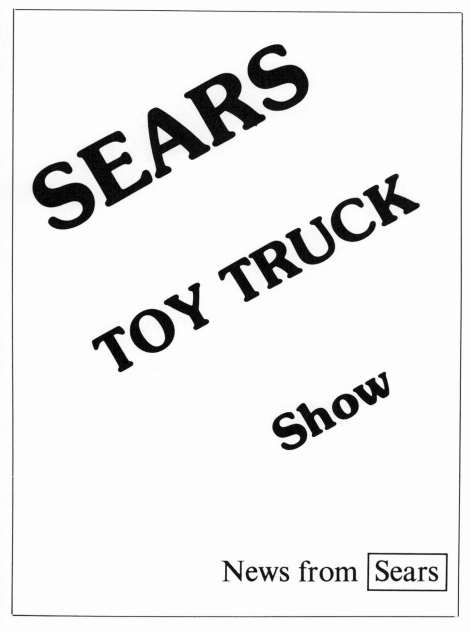

Figure 7-1.   Sears prepared a custom version of their usual press kit folder cover during their "Toy Truck Show," featuring small Toyota-size trucks, modified with Sears accessories.   (Courtesy Sears, Roebuck & Co.)

50th anniversary kit

FIFTY YEARS
OF
SUPERMARKETING

1930–1980

Food Marketing Institute, 1750 K Street, N.W. Washington, D.C. 20006

Figure 7-2. The Food Marketing Institute went to a custom press kit cover during their 50th anniversary of supermarketing promotion, incorporating the special computer bar code shopping basket logo. (Courtesy Food Marketing Institute)

154

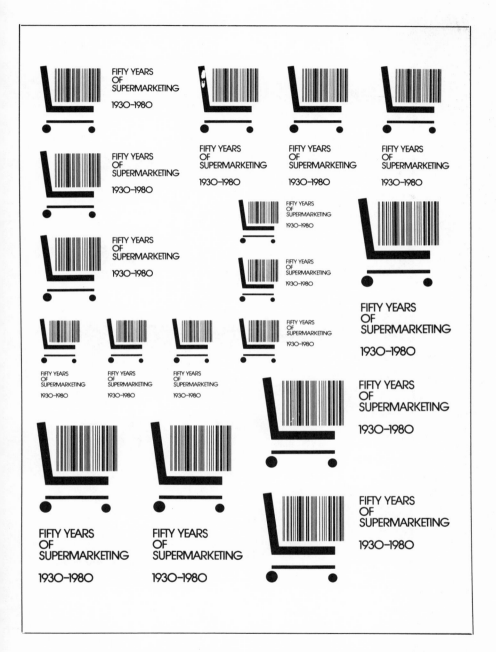

Figure 7-3.   The FMI anniversary logo was reproduced several times in different sizes on a "logo sheet" to make it easier for publications to reproduce, and included in the press kit.   (Courtesy Food Marketing Institute)

A GREAT AMERICAN INVENTION

This new kind of food outlet brought together self-service, mass merchandising and one-stop shopping. By drawing large numbers of customers, it could reduce prices by an average 25 percent and still stay in business.

Really nothing has changed. Supermarkets are still doing that today. But 50 years later they are such an established part of our daily lives that they're pretty much taken for granted.

The supermarket was invented just 50 years ago. What if it hadn't happened?

You, or whoever does your shopping, would need much more time—to buy bread from the bakery—meat from the meat market—fruit and vegetables from the produce store—and grocery items from the grocery.

Would that have had much of an effect on life in these United States—or even the world?

First, the cost of almost everything you put on the kitchen table would skyrocket because thousands of additional people would be necessary to service your needs. People like the butcher, the baker, the candlestick maker—each with his own staff of clerks to wait on you.

That's the way it was in 1930—before the first supermarket opened its doors in an abandoned garage during the depression. The supermarket, a product of hard times, helped the American people stretch their money a lot further.

The fact is, as a distribution system serving the public daily, the supermarket positively influences the quality and convenience of life as much as most significant inventions of the 20th century.

FIFTY YEARS
OF
SUPERMARKETING
1930–1980

Figure 7-4. Also in the FMI press kit was this prepared line art for a special box that publications were free to reproduce, as in feature or food sections of newspapers. Note the event logo at the bottom. (Courtesy Food Marketing Institute)

156

8

Special Coverage

There are special opportunities that may arise from the requirements of various publications, giving you a chance for extraordinary exposure. We'll be looking in this chapter at what those opportunities are, how to identify them, how to take advantage of them, and perhaps how to create them yourself.

Unlike most publicity programs where you try to appear in as many places as possible, these examples of special coverage require dealing with only one publication at a time. Fortunately, there are ways to capitalize on this coverage after the fact through a "broadside" (this term refers to any mass mailing to every name on a mailing list).

Of course, you may discover that there are enough causes for special coverage throughout the year to keep you very much in front of your most important audiences. It depends on how perceptive and quick to respond you can be. And it's all surprisingly easy. Shall we proceed?

Exclusives

The next time you have a major announcement to make, you might consider this simple expedient for gaining more than the usual amount of coverage. An *exclusive* is simply the right to your story before any other publication runs it. If you grant any one publication, chosen wisely from those most important to you, an exclusive, every other publication is free to pick up and run the same story later. An exclusive adds impetus and importance to your story and increases its chances of running (and with more space than might otherwise be the case).

The same magazines that are interested in your news when it's routine will be interested in giving special attention to your more important announcements.   These are generally the magazines closest to your industry, the business or trade publications that are most widely read by your colleagues and customers.   Within this broad category, your selection is best made by looking closely at the various individual publications.   Your best bet is one that's credible, and takes a special look at new announcements each issue.   Some   are merely inquiry-getters (not necessarily a bad thing).   Which do you think your audience holds in the highest regard?

Contact the editor who is responsible for the type of news you're reporting at each publication.   A glance at the editorial staff listings should help identify the proper "beat," or you can look for an editor's byline on the publicity exclusive in that issue.   Before you contact the editor, understand what it is you're offering, and what you may be called upon to provide—samples, photos, technical information, interviews with key personnel, etc.

Every publication in a competitive field enjoys scooping its competitors by running significant news stories first; for a variety of reasons, some dealing with sales positioning, others with sheer ego gratification. Many editors actively solicit sources of news, giving special attention to an important breaking story or announcement in exchange for the opportunity to publish it exclusively.

Usually, you're asked to make sure that no one publishes your news before they do, but they may request a week to a month advance period between the time they publish and the time that other media are notified.   Most of the time, the cover date of the issue is the determining factor, and you are free to place the same news anywhere else after that date.   The issue date, mailing date, or other factors may also influence the advance period.   Ask the editor you're dealing with for the lead time expected.   Or you can simply delay mailing your broadside releases until after your exclusive publication hits the stands.

With a big enough announcement, enough lead time, a lot of cooperation, and a little luck, you might even get your new product pictured on the cover.

Special Features

From time to time, and more often than you may think, magazines will offer special features on specific topics, which may or may not vary from year to year, month to month, or issue to issue.   These special features may include a substantial amount of research, or may be little more than aggregates of publicity releases on the subject.

In either case, any pertinent information you can provide has a good chance of appearing in the magazine's special feature,   provided you learn about it in time to get the pictures and information out.   This is one good reason to maintain a steady flow of releases to all pertinent editors.   There's often no telling when a   special feature will pop up, and you'll want a lot of your material to be on file, ready to pull and place.

But there are other things you can do to enhance your chances of appearing in special features.

The first is to be sure you know about them, and the best way to do this is to get hold of each publication's *editorial calendar*, a printed schedule of special features they're planning over the next   several issues, months, or year.   Editorial calendars are normally included in a publication's *media kit*, which is a package of materials they send to potential advertisers.   And herein lies an interesting   coincidence.

Has it occurred to you that the publications which you are most interested in for publicity are those that make the most sense for your company to advertise in?   This is not to suggest that you have to place ads to get publicity, nor that you should promise or even hint that an ad is forthcoming.   In fact, you may already be placing ads in these publications. It does, however, mean that somewhere in your company these editorial calendars may already be on file. Most publications aggressively approach potential advertisers, virtually thrusting promotional materials, including media kits and editorial calendars, upon them. So even if you don't advertise with them, chances are that most important publications will have already sent these materials to someone in your organization.

You may be wondering why editorial calendars would be included in promotional materials.   The answer is simple: Advertising a related product in an issue which is giving special attention to a product means reaching many readers with a specific interest in that product. Often, you'll find headlines like SPECIAL OPPORTUNITIES FOR ADVERTISERS   or SPECIAL OPPORTUNITY FOR (featured product) MANUFACTURERS AND SELLERS   on the editorial calendars inside media kits.

But what about those publications for whom you do not have media kits?   First, send this letter or one like it to the editors you have on your list:

Dear (name),

We are anxious to provide you with all possible support in your preparation of features concerning any
of our (product or services).   Since communication is
important in both directions, I am enclosing literature
about (product or services), and asking you to forward
a copy of your editorial calendar—or as much about
your future feature plans as you care to share.

Faithfully yours,

(signature, title)

As the responses come in, make a chronological tickler file
or special calendar as a reminder to request an updated editorial calendar two or three months before the one you have expires.
Next, look up the names of the publication's advertising sales representatives (or, lacking that, the publisher).   If you are the person
in your organization responsible for placing advertising, a direct request
for information is entirely suitable.   If not, chat with the advertising
person within your company about your needs and a joint plan of
action.   Send a letter something like this.

Dear (name),

I am (name), and I manage the publicity program
for (company).   Let me open by thanking you and your
editorial staff for being so very cooperative with our
publicity efforts.
Our advertising director, (name), has asked to be kept
up to date on the special features you are planning that
might involve our products (or services).   Toward that
end, I would like to ask you to keep us up to date with
regular mailings of your editorial calendar.
We are noting with enthusiasm the high interest your
readers appear to have in our products and activities.
While I am not certain of the specific advertising plans
at this time, I do know that we are growing and are
very interested in doing the best we can to reach new

customers effectively and efficiently. Being aware of special opportunities to reach them is an important part of our plan to achieve this goal, so I would like to thank you for your generous aid and assistance in cooperating with us.

Best regards,

(signature, title)

As you collect these editorial calendars, you will note one or two important deadlines.   The deadline for advertising reservations will be a later date than the deadline for literature, photos, and pertinent materials, usually predating it by about 30 days.   If only one deadline is stated, assume it is an advertising deadline.   If you want your publicity materials in the feature coverage, you'll have to beat that deadline by about a month.

This, by the way, would be an appropriate time to use the telephone to contact the individual to whom the special feature is assigned, learn the specific timetables, offer your assistance, and ask what literature, materials, or photography you can provide.   You may also want to offer to send product samples for their use in photography of related products.   And do whatever is needed to ensure that what you promise is delivered on or ahead of schedule.   If you must be a day or two later than you promised, you'll probably find that there's no problem, but you should certainly phone to announce and explain the delay.

To avoid last-minute aggravations, prepare your calendar or chronological file so that an entry is made for the date your materials are due, with a notation of the issue in which the coverage appears.   When working with the calendar, always look at least a month ahead of the current date to make sure you know what's coming and can prepare for it fully.

Hitchhiking

Many times you will discover that some feature coverage is planned that does not involve your company's products or services directly, but rather covers a related topic.   For example, if you manufacture an egg substitute, you may learn of an article about cholesterol.   If you manufacture birth control devices, you may discover features about changing morality, dating, or marriage versus careers.   If you manufacture bicycles, you may learn of features on the environment, the rising cost of energy, the trend toward living downtown, or what's new in physical fitness.   If you offer exercise classes, look for features about dieting, heart disease, mortality rates, keeping sexy, dressing, or grooming.   If you make lighting fixtures, you may learn of an article on new developments in light bulbs, how to combat crime, or land-scaping.

In each case, there's an opportunity for you to contact the editor or writer involved with the suggestion of a *sidebar*, which is the journal-istic term for material related, but not directly pertinent, to the sub-ject of an article.   A sidebar is usually presented either as a separate element on the side or bottom of the page, segregated from the main body of material, or in a box.

When you can prompt the inclusion of information about your products, services, or activities in this way, it is referred to as *hitch-hiking*, a term that is better known within the publicity profession than in the journalism profession.   The connotation is obvious and the results effective.

Focus Issues

Special features may involve a topic that is of such intense interest to the readers of a publication and of such complexity that no single article could do the topic justice.   In this case, a substantial group-ing of articles or even an entire issue may be devoted to a single topic and its various ramifications.   Whether the commitment is in whole or in part, these are referred to as *focus issues.*

A focus issue is the ink-and-paper equivalent of a forum, where a thorough discussion is invited and relevant comments encouraged. They provide, of course, a very encouraging opportunity for special coverage.

Focus issues may involve a number of different approaches to coverage, including product surveys, reviews of research and develop-ment activities, explanations of how a product is used, suggestions on how to shop intelligently for a product, information on the history of a product, and interviews with significant people in the industry.

Sounds a lot like the information you offer through your releases, doesn't it?

Your best approach here is again to contact the editorial people who are preparing these issues.   Talk about the coverage they're planning, offer your help, and suggest other ways you might be able to contribute.   This is an excellent opportunity to have articles authored by your people or ghostwritten for them, usually with full acknowledgment of the source.   It's also a great time to offer key people for interviews, and a prime opportunity to see your things on the cover.   You should have yourself a field day, professionally speaking.

Comparisons and Backgrounders

So far, we've been looking at ways in which you can respond to an editorial need.   The fact is, most publications, especially business publications, are hungry for good editorial material.   As a result, editors are almost always open to suggestions of ways in which good material might be prepared.   Here are some examples.

In your field, you have competitors.   How does the product you offer differ from the ones they offer?   If you can prepare a chart or list of all the pertinent information (operating parameters, specifications, size, weight, price, options—you know what's important to your customers), you have the core of an excellent article.   Find the best magazine to reach the people who buy these products and ask the editor about preparing a *comparison* article, covering not only your products, but all competing products as well.   Most editors appreciate that you're probably in a better position to know these things than they are.   They'll probably suggest that you include some basic text about what the various parameters mean, why they're important, and how to weigh the trade-offs in making a selection.   You (or an outside author) should prepare a story running about ten pages (typically—but ask the editor) of typed double-spaced manuscript. Submit it to the editor whose publication you've selected, after first phoning to query, of course.   Obviously, you can't talk down your competitors, but you can talk up the features you feel make your product or service a best choice for the buyer.

Backgrounders are another way of getting an article you prepare into print.   A backgrounder, as we discussed before, is an article that explains and illustrates the historical, technical, operational, or application background of a particular product or service.   Choose a subject and approach that you find fascinating, and chances are you will find an editor who is also interested in your story.   Again, query and ask advice as you have your article prepared.

Capitalizing on Special Coverage

Once that treasured article has appeared, your opportunity to take advantage of it has not at all disappeared.

One further advantage is to request (and pay for, if required) enough copies of the article to provide one or more for each of the people or organizations who sell your product or service. For a small company, this may amount to one copy to mount on a counter or a wall. wall.

Also, you should take this opportunity to obtain the publication's permission to reproduce the specific article or part of it or to buy *offprints* (the term for publication-prepared reproductions of the article alone). Then prepare a release that offers a copy of this article or coverage to inquiring readers, the same way you would offer any product literature.

Once again, your involvement in publicity requires that you be resourceful, imaginative, clever, thorough, and professional.

9

Results

What results do you expect from your publicity program? By now, you should have them clearly in mind. If publicity is only a means to your end, what do you still have to do? How do you do it?

There's a great deal more to conducting a successful publicity program than getting out releases. For most programs, this is just the beginning of a chain of events that leads to measurable results.

If it hasn't become apparent to you yet, you'll be happy to discover that you already know most of what there is to know about getting publicity. In these last two chapters we're going to discuss ways to put the publicity you generate to use, including ways to use your results to improve your results.

What Results?

What are the results—the *end* results—that you want your publicity program to achieve? This depends partly on the type of organization you're working for and the goals you've set for your publicity program. We've discussed many of these in other chapters, but let's review them here.

While we will try to be thorough in identifying all the various kinds of organizations for which you're likely to be conducting your publicity efforts, it's possible that your particular type of organization may not be covered here. Still, the categories presented are broad enough that you should be able to find one close to your own activities, and adapt the information to suit your own particular requirements.

Small Retail Operations

If you have a store or a small number of stores, whether you offer products or services, your business would most likely be categorized as a small retail operation.

Examples of small retail operations include grocery stores, supermarkets (we will be discussing *chain operations* separately), dry cleaners, laundromats, restaurants, service stations, hardware stores, clothing stores, notions stores, diet and exercise centers, private clinics (where the goal is primarily increasing the number of people who come to you—we'll discuss some other aspects of these under *charitable organizations* and *community service organizations*), stereo stores, appliance stores, furniture stores, shoe repair stores, camera stores, film processing operations, television repair businesses, car dealers, car washes, car parts stores, book stores, tobacco shops, produce markets, banks, equipment rental centers, card shops, newsstands, department stores, catalog showrooms, beauty salons, barber shops, computer stores, real estate agencies, insurance agencies, office supply stores, theaters, taverns, dating services, counseling centers (also discussed with community service organizations), trash haulers, lawn maintenance services, sewer cleaners, plumbers, legal services, antenna installers, dairies, bakeries, and so on.

These operations are typified by selling directly to the end user of the given products or services.   There is also direct contact with customers usually.   Most are not unique within a locale (normally, there are one or more competitors within the areas they serve), and all depend on their own sales for income, if not survival.

Publicity programs for small retail operations are capable of producing any or all of the following kinds of results:

1. *Increased awareness.*   How many times have you thought that business might be better if only more people realized you were there, or knew about everything you offer? Publicity can help make people more aware of you by giving you a higher profile; getting your name into print or on the air more often.   Studies have shown that most buying decisions are made on the basis of a selection between three or fewer alternatives, and it's hard to make the finals if no one knows you're competing.

2. *Increased traffic.*   *Traffic* is the term for the flow of people through your store, or the number of people contacting you.   Increased traffic usually means increased   sales

volume, mostly because people hate wasting a trip or their time and will often buy something just to justify their investment in time and trouble.   Publicity that merely increases awareness will prompt some increase in traffic, but an even greater increase in traffic can be realized if you implement something like a promotion   and   use publicity to help get the word out.

3. *Increased sales.* By using publicity to effectively communicate the benefits and features of the products or services you offer and the way you do business, you will be attracting customers who are looking for exactly what you're offering.   These may be customers currently doing business with your competitors, in which case you will be increasing your *share of market,*   the percentage   of all potential customers for what you offer who buy.   Or they may be customers who are now buying this type of product or service for the first time, in which case you are expanding your *customer base* or expanding the marketplace.   Either term means adding sales to your business without taking them away from your competitors, by selling to "new" people.

4. *Upgraded sales.*   Almost universally, the extra cost of a better product is more than justified by the added features, benefits, and value the customer receives.   And   also universally, you can make more money when you   sell a better product (compared to the basic or "economy" version).   Through publicity, you can communicate this value story to your customers.   The result is customers that are willing to spend a little more in order to get a little more.   In the vernacular, this is called "selling up;" officially, this is called *upgrading the sale.*

5. *Enhanced image.*   There may be a blockade between you and better sales in the form of an attitude held by a large portion of your potential customer base.   This attitude may be anachronistic, unfair, untrue, or unwarranted, but it is in any case prejudicial and detrimental to your business.   A specific example here may help illustrate how publicity can help solve this type of problem.

A few years ago, bowling proprietors discovered that they were missing out on a great many potential customers because their establishments had an image of being surly and male-dominated.   Women and children did not fit into the popular image. In addition, these places of business were known as "alleys," an outside ball ended up in the "gutter," and bowling balls were big, heavy, and black.

Well, the industry got together, changed "alleys" to "lanes" and "gutters" to "channels." They spruced up their facilities, introduced products and services aimed at attracting women, families, and "respectable citizens" (partly through community leagues), and communicated the striking transformation through a well-coordinated program of advertising, promotion, and publicity.

You can just as easily correct the record and the image of your business through a well-conceived and properly executed publicity program. And, as we've seen, a "not-what-you-think-it-is" angle on a story is one that editors are often open to.

There's no reason that your publicity program can't accomplish all of the above, if you're willing to make the investment in energy, time, and resources necessary to achieve them. But it's critically important that you limit the scope of your program to only those goals that you can reasonably accomplish. So choose carefully, choose wisely, and above all don't embark upon a publicity program without a specific plan of action.

Chain Operations

If your organization does business through a more substantial number of locations which are controlled by your business, either through direct ownership or some form of franchising, and these locations are themselves retail operations, your business would most likely be categorized as a *chain operation*.

Some examples of chain operations include fast food chains (McDonald's, Burger King, Kentucky Fried Chicken, Arthur Treacher's, Dairy Queen), restaurant chains (Howard Johnson's, Pizza Hut, Red Lobster, Bonanza, Brown Derby, Boar's Head, Dry Dock, Houlihan's, Ground Round, Stuckey's, Denny's, Big Boy), electronics chain stores (Radio Shack, Computerland, ComputerEase, Heathkit stores), chain hardware stores (Ace, Sentry), drug store chains (Rexall, Revco, CVS, Walgreen, Medic), supermarket chains (Kroger, Stop & Shop, A&P, Safeway, 7-11, Convenient, Wawa, Heinen's, Pathmark, PikQwik), department store chains (May Co., Sears, J.C. Penney, Marshall Fields), discount department store chains (Zayre, K Mart, Cook's, Clark's, Ontario, Uncle Bill's, Caldor, Woolco, Gold Circle), clothing store chains (Anderson-Little, T. J. Maxx, Dress Barn, Thom McAn, Chandler's, Florsheim, Shoe Town, Richman Brothers), specialty food chains (Hickory Farms, General Nutrition Center, Swiss Colony, Au Bon Pain, Carvel), chain pet stores (DoctoRx, Pet Land), and so on.

These operations can be characterized as selling directly to the end user of the given products or services.   There is usually direct contact with customers and the specific offerings at any one location will be similar or identical to those at any other location (and usually at similar or identical prices).   Chain stores compete with other retail or chain operations within a given locale, though seldom with other outlets of the same chain, and are supported by the common management of the chain in such areas as advertising, publicity, promotion, and purchasing.   While some of the income of each location may remain at that location (as in a franchise arrangement), a portion of the income from each location goes to the chain management, and survival of any one location does not necessarily depend on the sales income derived from that particular location.

Publicity programs for chain operations are capable of producing any or all of the following results:

1. *Increased awareness.*   As a chain grows, publicity can make more people aware of what it is and what it has to offer— both in new locations where customers may or may not already be aware of the chain, and in ongoing locations. Growth itself helps attract the attention of people and of larger-scope media.

2. *Increased traffic.*   Even more than with small retail operations, publicity can help increase people's curiosity about what a chain offers, particularly if there really is something there that their usual sources don't offer.   And since publicity can be accomplished on a larger scale (more regional and national media),   traffic-building promotions can be effectively communicated through publicity.

3. *Increased sales.*   Again, awareness and traffic inevitably lead to sales, though not necessarily at the same ratio of dollar-income-per-person-entering-place-of-business. Still, few businesses turn extra sales away.

4. *Upgraded sales.*   Chain operations generally offer a central group of products or services that remains fairly constant

and consistent.   There may be occasional variations in new products or services, however, which publicity can make people interested in.   Publicity can also keep customers aware of the upgrade products or services you offer, so while they may buy a basic version this first time, it will be easier to sell them a better version next time.

5. *Enhanced image.*   Some specific image problems that beset chain operations include the attitude that products, tools, or services are mass produced with corners cut to keep costs down and "big company" profits up.   The idea exists that customers are paying more than they need to in order to support "high rent" locations and aggressive advertising programs.   Store personnel may be seen as clerks with little or no expertise about the products or services being offered.

Publicity can help communicate the truth behind these fictions.   Education on the economies of   large volume purchasing, lower markups due to the greater number of sales in "high rent," high traffic locations, and training programs for store personnel can all help your image.

6. *Investor awareness.*   Chain stores are often publicly owned, their stocks traded on the open market at one of the exchanges or over the counter.   For investors, stock in your company is a product, and may be treated much like any other in making a buying decision.   Awareness of your activities and announcements can help build credibility in your company and faith in the way you do business.

7. *Employee morale.*   There's a certain pride that goes with seeing your company's name in print, especially when something nice is being announced.   And when the company does something nice for its employees, it's a very human reaction to feel a sense of satisfaction.   Good employee morale can help attract and keep good employees (important when you consider the cost of training), and help ease or even forestall labor negotiations if and when a union gets involved.

8. *Public relations.*   Public and community relations are more important than you may think at first glance.   Tax levels, zoning restrictions, and vandalism can all be reduced or avoided if the community believes you to be a good neighbor.   Publicity can help establish you as a concerned and

active member of the community, and help communicate your side of the story should problems arise.

9. *Franchise expansion.*   If your chain operation involves the sales of franchises, it's important to your growth that you attract the attention of the right kind of entrepreneur. While publicity isn't likely to screen applicants, it can generate enough good information about your activities and accomplishments to attract more good would-be investors (franchisees).

Here again, it's important to formalize your decisions about which of the above goals it's reasonable for your publicity program to try to accomplish.   Even though there's usually a little more money and a few more people available to help perform the publicity function within a larger organization (like the central management of a chain operation), your time and resources will still be limited.   So don't be discouraged by what you don't accomplish; appreciate that what you do accomplish is more than   could   have been   done   without publicity.

Distribution Operations

If your company does business with retail stores, but not directly with their customers, and you are not the manufacturer of the goods or service tools you sell, you would be considered a *distribution operation.*   Or your company may sell items it buys but does not manufacture to companies which use them in volume in their own manufacturing or processing of goods.   Your distribution operation   may also act as a middleman between a manufacturing company from which you buy and customers who are not generally the end users of your products.

Distribution operations go by several names, depending largely on the specific industry.   In some industries, there's an overlap between distribution operations and retail operations, since many distribution operations now occasionally also sell "over the counter" to some end users.   So, depending on the industry, a distribution operation may be known as a distributor, a warehouse operator, a distribution warehouse, a jobber, a stocking sales representative, a stock redistribution center, a distribution center, a redistribution center, and so on.

These operations seldom sell to the end user of a given product or service, but usually to someone who sells to the end user.   There is seldom contact with the end user and a substantial portion of all orders received are for large quantities.   In fact, a substantial portion of all orders placed are for very large quantities, and are placed directly with the manufacturers of these items.   It should be noted, especially for purposes of publicity, that many, if not most, distribution operations offer *value-added services*, meaning that some additional preparation, selection, or other service is performed on the stock items as a service to the businesses which buy from the distribution operation.

Publicity for distribution operations will most often be targeted toward business publications or the business pages of consumer publications, except where it is generated in the interest of public or community relations or employee morale.   Publicity is capable of producing the following kinds of results for distribution operations:

1. *Increased awareness.*   The most important category of potential customers for a distribution operation includes company purchasing agents and buyers, and publicity can help make sure that these people know about you and what you have to offer.   This includes any value-added services you provide.

2. *Increased traffic.*   Since most distributor operations don't deal with walk-in business, you are probably less concerned with increasing the number of walk-in customers than with increasing the number of people writing or calling to inquire about what you have to offer.   As we've mentioned, most publicity for distribution operations will be targeted toward those business publications that purchasing agents and other buyers are likely to read, and these are the publications that are very likely to offer readers' service inquiry forwarding.   With or without these inquiries, publicity can easily accomplish an increase in inquiries of other sorts, including requests for literature or quotations over the phone or through the mail.

3. *Increased sales.*   The ability to convert inquiries to sales depends in part on the talent of your sales personnel, but in any case will be enhanced by the dissemination of information that can be accomplished by or because of publicity.

4. *Upgraded sales.*   Within most distribution organizations, an upgraded sale means the sale of a larger quantity on any given order, since the cost of processing an order is a relatively fixed expense and much easier to amortize over a larger volume.   Publicity can be used to communicate

certain volume-sensitive promotions, such as special premiums offered at various volume levels.

5. *Enhanced image.*   Since most distribution organizations tend not to aggressively publicize their programs and business activities, those that do professionally communicate a well-executed flow of information tend to be regarded as "on-the-ball" leaders of their industry.   They are often better esteemed and regarded by potential customers, as well as current customers.   ("Hey, I do business with them," is a common feeling of pride and of being among the aware elite of buyers.)   Publicity can also help accomplish the improvement of an operation's image as a business within the community.

6. *Investor awareness.*   Most distribution operations are not self-capitalizing, meaning that they have to depend on banks and financial institutions for lines of credit and other forms of banking.   Some may "go public" and issue stock instead.   In either case, a progressive image can help favorably impress investors and funding sources, making the operation's financial life a little easier.   Publicity can help accomplish this image.

7. *Employee morale.*

8. *Public relations.*   As citizens of the local business community, subject to the vagaries of regulations, taxation, and enforcement, good public and community relations can be worth a lot more than a good feeling when you go to bed at night.

Since distribution operations tend to require minimal operational overhead, they tend not to be involved with very extensive publicity programs.   So whatever efforts you are able to make must be extremely efficient if they are to be effective.   Ask yourself what kind of results are most important to your operation.   Which are the most urgent?   Tailor your program to accomplish those results *specifically*, remembering that there will be a happy byproduct for all your efforts.

Manufacturers

If you produce end products that are assembled or converted from less sophisticated materials, you are a *manufacturer*.   While manufacturing may be incidental to your other operations (some distribution operations, for example, manufacture unique products to meet specific customer demands, and find the products in demand by many other customers), if your end product is eventually made available for sale to an end user outside of your organization, our discussion here applies.

Processors and reprocessors may also be considered manufacturers in this sense. If what you do is clean, inspect, and package fruit, consider yourself a manufacturer for the purposes of our discussion. If you form ground beef into hamburgers and package it for sale through the frozen food departments of groceries and convenience stores, you're included too. If you import goods and relabel them, repackage them, provide domestic language documentation, or have this all accomplished for you by the people you buy from, you can also count yourself in. The same applies if your product is information, which you package as books, tapes, records, custom computer programs, magazines, telephone services, or many other forms. If what you package is an original service—like those of graphic arts studios, advertising agencies, marketing research consultants, testing firms, and so on—you're also included. No matter how broadly manufacturing is defined, most of the results we discuss can be accomplished by a publicity program.

1. *Increased awareness.*

2. *Increased traffic.* This is accomplished through the various ways in which potential customers or clients can find out what you have to offer; by seeing you or your products or services, by telephone inquiries, by mail inquiries, and so on.

3. *Increased sales.* Increased sales to the end user through any forms of distribution or representation may be realized. Increased sales to current and added channels or outlets of distribution or sales are also included.

4. *Upgraded sales.* This includes both increased quantities to quantity buyers (like distribution, business, and industrial customers) and the sale of better (more expensive) versions to end users.

5. *Enhanced image.*

6. *Investor awareness.*

7. *Employee morale.*

8. *Public relations.*   This includes community relations, of course, for all those communities in which your facilities are located.

9. *Distribution expansion.*   If there are middleman operations of any kind (in other words, if you do not sell direct to the end user exclusively), adding to the number of such operations you deal with can mean a significant increase in your business.   This is especially true if you can add distribution into industries or geographic areas you have not effectively reached before.   Publicity directed to those publications that are read by distribution organizations within these areas and industries (as well as your own) can help generate interest in what you have to offer.   This is also true for representation in businesses and industries where manufacturer's representative organizations are well established.

Depending on the size and liquidity of your organization, you may be able to design a publicity program that accomplishes all of the above and more.   In designing such a program, it's mandatory that you evaluate each release and activity that you plan in terms of its role in each of the above areas.   It's no good, for example, crying poverty to labor organizations when you're bragging about success to business editors.   Organize before you execute and you'll find that you can accomplish everything you set out to do.   It's easier than it sounds.

Civic, Charitable, Cultural, and Non-Profit Organizations

An organization is considered non-profit if it depends on donations from people and businesses who believe in what it's doing and support it through voluntary contributions.   There is no direct return of goods or services as a result of such expenditure. For the purpose of our discussion, a number or organizations that aren't normally con- sidered charitable organizations will be included here as well.   For example, a non-commercial public television station may not usually be considered a charity, but will considered one here. So will scholar- ship funds, research organizations dedicated to eliminating specific afflictions or diseases, charity hospitals, youth organizations like

Scouting and the Y.M.C.A./Y.W.C.A., churches and religious institutions, private, non-profit organizations concerned with the needs of the disabled, the elderly, the destitute, the infirm, and other disadvantaged members of our society, and most other activities that raise funds that are redistributed to persons who need them.

In terms of publicity, these organizations most often need support of fund-raising activities, and may also need communication to help establish to the community at large that these services or facilities are available.   Here are some results publicity programs   may   be designed to accomplish.

1. *Increased awareness.*   Charitable organizations   are   interested in reaching the   most people with information about the special services or facilities they make available. Publicity (in concert with public service announcements and donated advertising space and time) can be an effective way of accomplishing this.   It's of course in the best interest of these organizations that as many potential donors and benefactors as possible are fully aware of their good deeds and need for contributions.   These contributions, by the way, are not at all limited to cash.   Many organizations involve themselves with the redistribution of donated food, the repair of mended donated household goods, the repair and sale of donated clothing, the redistribution of donated eyeglasses and hearing aids or other prosthetic aids and appliances, the redistribution of donated blood, tissue, or body organs, and so on. In each case, a continued supply of donations depends on the awareness and good will of the public, and publicity is capable of helping accomplish this.

2. *Increased participation.*   The "traffic" of a charity can be the number of people involved in volunteer work, the number of people involved in the volunteer solicitation of contributions, or the number of people reached by such efforts.   Publicity can help disseminate a call for volunteers of either type, while alerting the public to such solicitations or related activities.

3. *Increased donations.*   The more people you make aware of your activities, of why you're conducting them, of the benefits your organization offers, and of other motivations for donations, the better your donations will be.   These, of course, are all jobs publicity can readily accomplish.

4. *Upgraded donations.*   The person who is already predisposed   toward support of your efforts can be persuaded,
via the messages and reports you share through publicity,
to increase the level of his or her contribution.   Often,
this is a more practical route to increased support than
attempts to reach larger numbers of possibly less favorably
inclined people.

5. *Enhanced image.*   Almost every charitable organization
has sometime heard, "It's just a big rip-off—all the money
goes into the directors' pockets or into fancy advertising."
Regardless of where these myths originate, publicity can
help set the record straight.   Also, publicity is a "cleaner"
promotional and communications channel than advertising, since the public is generally aware that publicity costs
nothing.

6. *Sponsor awareness.*   Many charitable organizations derive
substantial portions of their financial support from a
limited number of individuals, foundations, or businesses.
While the good will and support of these sponsors are virtually assured, publicity can be used to reach them with
reports of your activities and good works, giving them a
continuing sense of satisfaction and   encouraging their
continued sponsorship.

Charitable organizations enjoy several advantages and opportunities
that many other publicity-generating organizations cannot share. For
example, many professional publicity agencies are pleased to donate
their services in support of your activities.   Many of the businesses
sponsoring your charitable works will likewise make their people or
facilities available to you.   There are also favorable postage rates (some
free, but check with your local postal officials) available to non-profit
organizations.   And volunteer workers, while sometimes unreliable,
are nevertheless almost always available to whatever degree you require
them.

All of this puts more of a burden on the planning, management,
and administration of a publicity program than on its actual execution.
If your publicity work is in support of a non-profit charitable organization, you are certain to find your work especially challenging, satisfy-
ing, and rewarding.

Community and Community Service Organizations

Community organizations is a category we will use to include community clubs, groups, and associations, or organizations made up of people with some common interest.   This common interest may be a hobby or avocation, experiential (as in veterans' organizations), participatory (including anything from Little League and bowling leagues to little theater and chess or bridge clubs), geographic (block organizations, for example), age-related (golden age associations or young people's groups), or related to the activities of specific family members (as with the P.T.A. or auxiliaries).

Community service organizations are those community organizations which exist to provide needed services to their communities on a non-profit basis.   Examples of such organizations include Knights of Columbus, Masons, B'nai B'rith, Rotary, Lions, Elks, Eagles, Welcome Wagon, and so on.

These organizations tend to use publicity sparingly and generally for one of the following results.

1. *Increased awareness.*

2. *Increased community attendance at sponsored functions.*

3. *Increased membership.*

4. *Enhanced image.*

There is one caveat to your involvement in your group's publicity program, of whatever size. If you can be left on your own to accomplish what you need to do (within whatever budget is set for you), you'll find it much less frustrating than if releases and mailing lists must be compiled by committee.   Report when it's done and show any results like clippings from a local paper.

Government Organizations

A great many governmental agencies conduct extensive publicity programs in support of their various activities.   While the variety of such organizations is as vast as the variety of all other organizations that may be conducting publicity programs, there are some differences worth noting.

Few if any government organizations are concerned with generating sales of goods or services.   However, they are concerned with the proper utilization of these goods or services, and with cooperation with the public and industry (for example in the proper filing of necessary forms as well as in the dissemination of findings).   They generally seek a broadly-based understanding and support of their functions, on which their budgets often depend.

So, for government agencies and organizations, the following kinds of results are most likely to be sought:

1. *Increased awareness.*   It's important for the people and organizations who will eventually interact with an organization, as well as for the public at large, to understand what an agency does, how it does it, why it does it, whom it does it for, and so on.

2. *Increased proper utilization.*   It is often difficult for a government agency to know or contact everybody who should be using their services.   For example, the Veterans' Administration had for some time been trying to reach those veterans who might have been exposed to Agent Orange in Viet Nam for examination and possible treatment, but up to recently only a small proportion of those who might have been exposed were aware of this.   And the Federal Communications Commission is offering refunds to amateur radio operators who paid for their licenses during a specific period in the seventies, but only a small portion have applied.   The more government services are properly used and applied, the greater the reason for continuing them (and the less the chance they'll be discontinued).   Obviously, publicity can be an invaluable ally in this effort.

3. *Increased participation and recruitment.*   Many government organizations, especially the military, have a continuing requirement for qualified personnel.   Publicity can help communicate the needs, rewards, and opportunities associated with each job, and keep a flow of applications from interested individuals.

4. *Enhanced image.*   One of the most keenly felt image problems in government is the sense of impersonal treatment, despite tremendous efforts by the government to counteract this.   Is the IRS person who helps prepare

an individual's return looking for things to report for later investigation?   Probably not;   most are sincerely interested in helping to untangle the mathematical maze and seeing that all eligible deductions are taken.   Is the county clerk just collecting names to pass on to pals who sell aluminum siding and life insurance?   Probably not;   it's more likely a case of providing records to substantiate an individual's status for other organizations within local government, to confirm eligibility for specific programs.   Recent reports in the media claim that one out of every three working people is employed by government—that's a lot of helping hands and a lot of good people, and publicity can do a lot to   help us all understand   the things they do for us.

5. *Employee morale.*   Publicity can reach not only those people who can use a service or want to know about a service, but those people who perform the service as well. And when their good works   are in   the spotlight, morale gets a boost.

There are many parallels between government organizations and the other operations we've discussed.   By now, you should have a fairly thorough understanding of the similarities, as well as the differences. In fact, we will consider only one more category before we   move on.

Political Issues and Candidates

Whether your publicity program is in support of a candidate who's running for dogcatcher, a school official, or a Presidential candidate, there's only one result that's going to make any difference: votes. Consider these ballots the currency with which your issue or candidate will be paid, and apply what you know about using publicity to help sell any other product or service.   The key selling points are going to be the relative benefits of your issue, should it pass   or   be   defeated (depending on which side you're on), or your candidate.   And, of course, you can   "tip the scales"   by encouraging the right kind of "traffic"—making sure the people who support you get out and vote.

Additional Information

If the results you seek from your publicity program include sales, votes, or attendance, you are probably going to want to consider having additional information at the ready to send to anyone who inquires as a result of your publicity efforts. A carefully tailored grouping of pertinent information should be available with a more complete description of you, your products or services, prices, details on availability and whatever else is appropriate. This is called a *fulfillment package.*

The fulfillment package is generally used as the second step (publicity being the first) in a program to achieve the end results you have decided to pursue. While there is no way to control how much information will be communicated in the coverage that results from your releases, you do have full control over the amount and quality of information you provide in a fulfillment package.

In fact, many organizations include a "bounce-back," postage-paid reply card in their fulfillment packages, inviting the inquirer to inquire again, usually for information about other available products or services. And some include descriptions and literature about everything they offer, regardless of the specific product interest that triggered the inquiry.

Here is a list of the kinds of literature you may want to consider including in your fulfillment package:

1. Cover letter. ("Thank you for your interest.")

2. Product literature, including specification sheets, descriptions of options, and accessories.

3. Reprints of favorable press reviews.

4. Application notes.

5. Price sheets.

6. Distributor lists or ordering information.

7. Line card (a sheet describing whatever else you offer).

8. Bounce-back card.

If you are not selling directly to the person or organization making the inquiry, but to an operation (such as a retailer or distributor) that will sell directly to the inquirer, it's also a good idea to forward a copy of the inquiry for follow-up.

If you are maintaining a mailing list of potential sales prospects for the future, you should also arrange for the routine inclusion of these inquiries on your list.

Some organizations follow up the fulfillment package a few weeks later with a second mailing; usually a letter or card asking if the materials have been received, if they were adequate, if the prospect intends to purchase, or attend, or vote your way, as appropriate, and if there's anything else you can send or do.

If your organization is a small one, you may not have the opportunity to follow up with this thoroughness. If it is a large one, this follow-up may be accomplished by other people in the sales or marketing departments. In any case, it's important for all the people involved in soliciting and servicing inquiries to understand all the steps of the process—if for no other reason than to appreciate your role in generating a substantial number of new leads through publicity.

Using Results To Create Stories

The publicity cycle goes full circle when you use the results of your efforts as the springboard for new releases. A few headlines may help illustrate how this is done.

> "XYZ Company reports unprecedented interest in new light bulb"

> "Customer interest in (your product or service) at an all-time high"

> "Public wants to know more about (whatever), reports XYZ"

> "New (whatever) drawing media spotlights"

In publicity, you see, old stories never die, and with a little attention, seldom fade away. They become new stories, with a life of their own, like the Phoenix rising from its own ashes to be reborn.

Yes, it means more work. But if you didn't already love the excitement and satisfaction of getting publicity, you wouldn't have reached the beginning of our final chapter.

10

Success!

Just a moment now! You may or may not be on the brink of conducting a successful publicity program. But what makes a publicity program successful? We've just reviewed the kinds of results you may be planning for your program to achieve, but how can you gauge the relative success or failure of your efforts?

There are certain successes you can measure: These include success in gaining overall coverage, success in gaining coverage in specific publications, and success in conducting a program efficiently.

Tracking Release Placement

One measure of success you can easily make is how much space or time your program achieves. There are both crude and refined methods of keeping track of this.

The crudest method is a file or scrapbook of clippings you happen to catch in the various publications you receive. (You might want to subscribe to the most important titles on your list, but this can quickly become very expensive.) A logbook or file of notes will also keep track of broadcast coverage you happen to hear or hear about.

But there's help available for this monitoring process in the form of professional reading and clipping services. Some of the largest are Luce (they have offices in several major cities; if not listed in your phone directory, try contacting their Washington, D.C. office at 202-783-1650), Bacon's (contact their Chicago office at 312-922-8419), and Burrelle's Press Clipping Bureau (75 East Northfield Avenue, Livingston, NJ   07039). These services generally charge a moderate monthly fee, plus a small fee for each clipping they pull.

In order to keep track of your program at a moderate cost, you will probably want to limit the number of publications they monitor for you.   For example, if you have a story that gets picked up by a wire service and subsequently by a large number of daily newspapers, and these are all clipped by the service, that one story could easily cost you well over a hundred dollars.

The best bet is to give the clipping service a list of the specific magazines you want monitored, plus a limited number of newspapers— including, perhaps, the local newspapers from the localities where your facilities are located, or newspapers within a limited geographic region.

Clipping services will pull all releases that contain any key words you request.   You may want to include your company name and brand names, trademarks and service marks, or some less comprehensive listing.   You might also consider asking them to clip only those placements that include pictures, which will reduce the comprehensiveness of the return somewhat but still give you an overall look at the coverage you're getting.

The advantages of comprehensive clippings are manifold. They provide, even at first glance, direct and tangible evidence of the results of publicity.   They give you a way of seeing what kinds of releases are most likely to get picked up by which kinds of publications. They tell you the likelihood of given groups of people being aware of specific kinds of information.   And they tell you which publications need more attention if your releases aren't appearing in them.

By the way, if you have the money available, you may want to consider asking a clipping service to also forward clips of stories that run about your competitors.   Many sophisticated organizations do this to keep track of what their competitors are up to, and to help stay responsive to new developments in the marketplace.

No matter what or whom you track, it's important to maintain a highly organized approach to record-keeping.   While we are about to suggest one proven technique for doing so, it is by no means the only technique and you are encouraged to develop one that best suits your particular requirements.

There are some things you're going to want to enter into your records for each clip you receive:

    1. In which publication did it appear?   This information will usually appear on a small piece of paper to which the clipping is attached.   If you have provided a unique code number for each publication on your publicity mailing list (a good idea, especially if you don't always mail a release to the entire list), you can use this code to identify

the publication.   You may also want to include the issue date or the date you receive the clipping.

2. Which release prompted the story?   If you number your releases, this code can help you keep abreast of what came from where.   In fact, you may want to keep duplicate files; one organized by publication, the other by release.

3. How much coverage did you get?   Maybe you don't care, and only want to list that the story appeared.   Or maybe you do, in which case the best quantitative measure is the number of column-inches the story occupies.   Column-inches are determined by measuring the length (in inches) of each column of the story and adding them.   You will want to include the headline in this measurement, and may or may not want to include photos.

4. Were any pictures included?   You can record the number of pictures, of course, as well as the number of column-inches the pictures occupy.   You may also want to include a code to indicate whether the pictures were black-and-white (the letter "B," for example) or color (the letter "C").

One of the most difficult things about keeping track of placements is learning the self-discipline of attending to your record-keeping (which can be very tedious if you're very successful).   It takes time to decide which release prompted a given story, and the fresher that release is in your mind, the better your chances are of being accurate. Also, the more you put off the task, the more ominous it is, so try to record each one as it's received.

Interpreting the Placement Record

Okay, now that you've done such a wonderful job of compiling all this data, what good is it?

Let's look at some specific interpretations of your clipping records and see what kind of information you can expect to extract from them. While you can perform these evaluations at any time, they're most valuable if performed no more often than quarterly; otherwise you may not be dealing with a complete record.   No less often than annually is best; otherwise you may be dealing with old and at least partially invalid data.

Publication Scores by Par

When evaluating your results, freeze them by opening a new file for record-keeping purposes and work only with clippings recorded as of a stated cut-off date.   If not, your task will be as frustrating as trying to bail out a rowboat with a hole in its bottom during a thunder-shower.

Pull the records on each publication for which any releases at all have been reported.   Place the records for all other publications in a special file marked "NO-SHOWS" to deal with separately (we'll explain how below).

Count the number of publications for which results have been reported.

Next, for each of these publications, add up all the column-inches and the total number of pictures reported during this evaluation period. Mark this total at the top of the page in colored pen or pencil.   Each page will then have something like "1641-3-34" at the top (for column-inches and pictures).

Next add up the grand total for all of these publications.   This figure reflects the total publicity coverage you received during the specific period of time your records cover.

Divide these grand total figures by the total number of publications in which publicity has appeared (which you determined a few steps ago).   This figure is the average coverage you received in each publica-tion.

Now a bit of math is required.   You are going to be expressing the coverage of each publication as a   percentage of the average cover-age.   There will be separate calculations for column-inches and for pictures.   Here's the formula:

$$\frac{\text{Individual Publication Total}}{\text{Average Coverage}} \times 100 = \text{Percentage of Average Response (P.A.R.)}$$

Scores for each publication in each category (space in column-inches and pictures) will vary from a few percent to a few hundred percent. The *percentage of average response* (P.A.R.) scores are an excellent indicator of how well you are reaching that particular publication.

Next, arrange a list of these publications, ranked in the order of their par scores, from highest to lowest.   We'll discuss what to do with this list later.

Release Scores by Par

Follow this procedure for each release.   First, calculate the total amount of space and the total number of pictures each release has gained.   Second, divide the total for all releases by the number of releases to determine the average space and the average number of pictures each release has earned   (which you've done above, so don't duplicate your own effort).   Include the letter   "N"   or the code "N/A" in the picture column if no picture was included in the mailing. Then calculate the par score for each release, once for space and again for pictures.   And finally, rank them in order of their par scores, from highest to lowest, on two lists—one for space, one for pictures.

Coding Publications by Type

When you first established your mailing list, you chose different groups of publications in order to accomplish different kinds of goals, or to reach different groups of readers.   Devise a simple code for yourself that identifies these groups of publications, like "W" for women's or "CR" for car repair.   Note these codes next to the par scores on each of the two publication lists.

You may notice that you do extremely well in reaching certain groups and poorly in reaching others.   This is to be expected.   In fact, you probably could have forecasted which would do the best when you first compiled your mailing list.   Look for publications that aren't scoring like others in their group; if one of a group scores much more poorly or much better than others.   Flag these entries with some kind of distinctive marking—perhaps a star for overachievers and a question mark for underachievers.

Coding Releases by Type

Your habits and tendencies in writing releases are by now fairly well established, and each time you begin you know what you are about to write.   Again, give yourself a simple code for each type of release you do, like "NP" for new product,   "PP" for personnel and pro-motions, "NL" for new literature, and so forth.

Review your file of releases that are included in this evaluation and mark each with an appropriate code.   You may notice that there are groupings of releases of specific types; flag those that show par scores much different from others of the same group.

Also, if you offer different kinds of products or services, you may want to code your release results with labels for each category.   Flag those examples that vary from the typical, as before.

What To Do About It

For those publications with a par score above 100, and for those publications that score better than others in their group, send a letter to each editor and individual on your list telling him of your review and thanking him for such splendid cooperation.

For those publications with a par score below 20-30, and for those publications that score much worse than others in their group, send the individuals on your list a letter asking if there isn't some way you could work more closely to improve your editorial relationship.

For those publications in your "NO-SHOWS" file, send a letter asking if for some reason you might have missed seeing their coverage of your news.   Ask if there's some reason they feel it's inappropriate to relay your news and offer your help to establish a closer working relationship.   Depending on their response and on their past or future scores, you may want to consider dropping them from your mailing list.   By the way, it's possible you've been sending your materials to a bad address or a publication that's out of print, so double check their listings in at least *two* media directories.

In short, if a publication doesn't perform up to par, the professional response is not to be angry with them, but to service them, nurture them, even romance them.

In reviewing the results of your placements by release, you may "discover" some phenomena you already know about.   For example, few publications go out of their way to pick up releases about person- nel and promotions, and most publications are more interested in the first announcement of a new product than in any other kind of release.

But more important, you may discover some phenomena that will help you greatly improve your publicity program.

For example, if releases about one specific type of product are picked up much less often than the others, it's possible that you're missing its biggest potential audience.   Talk to the people who buy or sell that product about who's likely to use it and how it's likely to be used.   You might even ask them where they think they're most likely to read about products like it.   Then hit the directories again and see if you can come up with additional publications for your mailing list.

If you find that a specific type of release for a specific product does better than most (for example, "quotes" releases or application stories), you've identified a "hot" topic that you can continue to exploit heavily by continuing to send more of the same kind of release.

And you may find that some types of releases do so poorly that they really aren't worth the effort.   In that case, don't waste your future efforts on them.   By the way, before you assume that a release is doing poorly, double check the date it went out.   If it's fairly recent, the bulk of its coverage may still be forthcoming.

In short, your review of results by release can help you run your program at peak efficiency and with a minimum of waste.

Was It Worth It?

Like many other fields where intense personal involvement is required, where results are difficult to measure immediately, where a lot of what you do is based on guesswork and imagination, people who conduct publicity programs develop a certain intuition for when things are going right, when things are going wrong, and how well it will all turn out in the end.

Trust that intuition.

Keep an eye on the results you've planned to achieve.   Are they happening?   Have you been an important part of making them happen? How could you not have!   Publicity is a formal marketing communications discipline that's been proven to work almost since whoever-it-was coined a name for it.

And now you've been introduced to the ins and outs of sharing that news of yours we talked about at the very beginning.   Are you ready? Do you feel a little better prepared than before we started?

You should.   Because now you know what the professionals know.

It's always worth it.

Index